THOSE EARLIER HILLS

This page: Raymond M. Patterson
in his garden, Victoria, BC.

Those Earlier Hills
Reminiscences
1928 to 1961

R.M. Patterson

From *The Beaver, Canada's History Magazine*

Victoria • Vancouver • Calgary

TouchWood Editions
#108–17665 66A Avenue
Surrey, BC V3S 2A7
www.touchwoodeditions.com

TouchWood Editions
PO Box 468
Custer, WA
98240-0468

Library and Archives Canada Cataloguing in Publication

Patterson, R. M. (Raymond Murray), 1898–1984.

Those earlier hills : reminiscences 1928 to 1961 / R.M. Patterson.

Includes bibliographical references.

ISBN 978-1-894898-67-6 (bound).—ISBN 978-1-894898-80-5 (pbk.)

1. Patterson, R. M. (Raymond Murray),—1898–1984—Travel—Canada, Northern.
2. Patterson, R. M. (Raymond Murray),—1898–1984—Travel—Canada, Western.
3. Canada, Northern—Description and travel. 4. Canada, Western—Description and travel. 5. Frontier and pioneer life—Canada, Northern. 6. Frontier and pioneer life—Canada, Western. I. Title.

FC75.P38 2008   917.1204'2   C2007-907440-5

Library of Congress Control Number: 2008921286

Edited by Marlyn Horsdal
Proofread by Meaghan Craven
Cover design: Frances Hunter
Section photos: page xii The Falls of the Nahanni, page 62 A Wolverine skin, page 100 The Nahanni
Printed in Canada by Friesens

BRITISH COLUMBIA
ARTS COUNCIL
Supported by the Province of British Columbia

Canada Council   Conseil des Arts
for the Arts   du Canada

TouchWood Editions acknowledges the financial support for its publishing program from the Government of Canada through the Book Publishing Industry Development Program (BPIDP), Canada Council for the Arts, and the province of British Columbia through the British Columbia Arts Council and the Book Publishing Tax Credit.

This book has been produced on 100% post-consumer recycled paper, processed chlorine free and printed with vegetable-based dyes.

"My whole life has been passed within sight of hills . . . Even now, as I write, I see [the mountains of the Buffalo Head] once again—blue-shadowed, outlined in gold against the setting sun . . . They were my friends. Those earlier hills were but my pathway to them."

—R. M. Patterson, *The Buffalo Head*

This page: "Those earlier hills . . ."

Contents

Foreword

A Google search for "Nahanni River" today returns over 30,000 website references, most of which offer exclusive canoe and rafting tours on the river. Conquering "the dangerous river" remains as much of an adventurer's challenge today as it was for Raymond Murray Patterson in 1927, and the wonders of the Internet make it easy for travellers to sample the experience before they book their flights. At the time Patterson wrote, such adventure travel was mostly the stuff of lifelong dreams. For many, his vivid written accounts and breathtaking photography were the perfect ticket to transport them to the sounds and smells of the Nahanni.

R.M. Patterson was a regular contributor to the then-quarterly, Hudson's Bay Company-published *The Beaver: Magazine of the North* and he worked with two of the magazine's longest-serving editors, Clifford P. Wilson and Malvina Bolus. Back then, as the subtitle implied, the magazine mostly featured stories of exploration of Canada's North, both historic and contemporary. Patterson was the quintessential *Beaver* contributor, always delivering a compelling story that seamlessly wove together historical reflection and modern experience. His work appeared in virtually every issue of the magazine over a period of 25 years, or "outfits," as they are called, because *The Beaver* is still organized according to the numbers of years the HBC has been in the fur trade.

One of the great pleasures for collectors of Canada's second-oldest magazine is the timeless appeal of its feature articles. Over the past few years our staff have talked often about ways to make our story archives more accessible, especially to those who may not be safeguarding a complete set in their home library. This first-time collaboration with TouchWood Editions provides an opportunity for non-*Beaver* collectors to discover the wealth of stories of one of its most popular writers, and we are excited about introducing R.M. Patterson to a wide variety of new and appreciative readers.

As for the quest for the next generation of R.M. Pattersons—today's *Beaver*, now published by Canada's National History Society, continues with the same editorial dedication to bring Canada's stories to life through lively writing and visual representations. We invite you to discover this new era of history's storytellers for yourself. Copies of *The Beaver: Canada's History Magazine*, and our new children's comic book-styled magazine, *Kayak: Canada's History Magazine for Kids*, are available by subscription and wherever fine magazines are sold in Canada.

Deborah Morrison
President and C.E.O
Canada's National History Society
March 2008, Outfit 339

The Nahanni Country

River of Deadmen's Valley

The Beaver, June 1947

The word "Nahanni" means "People of the West." The country too was given a name, by an American—a man with a dash of the poet in his makeup—who came and was conquered by the fantastic beauty of it in a rain-washed summer of blue skies and sudden storms. He called it "The Land of Shadows." Jack London must have heard about it when, years ago, in *Smoke Bellew*, he ran his man "beyond all outer charting" into the country of the Divide, beyond the headwaters of the Pelly. There Bellew was captured by the Montagnais Indians—the Mountain Men—and brought in to the old white man and his daughter who ruled over them.

This "White Chieftainess" (sometimes with a necklace of coarse gold) crops up persistently. Robert Campbell, in his autobiography, tells how he met the chieftainess of the Nahannis in July 1838. Hal G. Evarts got hold of the yarn, on a trip down the Yukon, and wrote *Moccasin Telegraph*. John Buchan, Lord Tweedsmuir, heard of the Nahanni legend as he went down the Mackenzie to the Arctic. Helge Ingstad, in his book, *Land of Feast and Famine*, mentions a party of trappers, hundreds of miles away in the Slave River country, yarning around the campfire about the canyons, the gold and the lost men. They had never seen the South Nahanni, but old Al Greathouse had touched the fringes of it and told them a

Facing page: A.J. La Flair's trading post.

3

thing or two. And Michael Mason, F.R.G.S., mentioned it in his book, *The Arctic Forests*. A strange country, he said it was, kept inviolate by the Nahannis, who "are hostile to strangers and many white pioneers have been done to death by them." This last remark, coming in a serious book, seemed, in the year 1926, worth looking into. Also, the doctor had ordered me, for a year at least, to do no heavy work. A canoe trip seemed to be the thing—down the Mackenzie, up the Liard, up the Nahanni as far as possible and out, in the late fall, by Fort Nelson and the Peace. Later on, struggling the canoe, solo, up the Nahanni, or humping a large pack south toward the Peace in October, I often thought with a grin of that rather pompous surgeon and his careful recommendations.

So I got together an outfit, and finally, after many vicissitudes, my canoe and I landed up on a July evening of 1927 at South Nahanni, the Indian village close under Nahanni Butte, where the Nahanni meets the Liard. There arrived also, that evening, Albert Faille (pronounced "Faley"), a Wisconsin trapper of Swiss descent and, simultaneously, an appalling thunderstorm. We sought shelter in A.J. La Flair's trading post and fought mosquitoes by means of a smudge in the doorway—a two-edged weapon, we found, as we groped and spluttered over our supper. Later, we fixed up

Facing page: Raymond Patterson at the Twisted Mountain, 1927. This photograph was taken by Albert Faille.

our mosquito nets, and lay and talked, and let the mosquitoes enjoy the cabin in peace. For me, a three-year association with a very wonderful and beautiful river had begun.

Now there are good maps, from aerial surveys, of the

Nahanni and its big tributary, the Flat River. In 1927–29 we had none of these aids to navigation—there were only two straight lines on the maps (each in the wrong place, one discovered later), and on the Nahanni line, about 120 miles up, the magic word "falls."

Starting upstream from South Nahanni, you have first some ten miles of slack water, where the river meanders silently round two oxbows. Nahanni Butte appears, mirrored in the calm waters, from every possible angle. "This," you think, "is not so bad."

You don't think that for very long. For the next 20 miles or so you have the Splits to deal with—a maze of channels and islands, sandbars, shingle bars, sweepers and huge driftpiles— an annoyance in low water, a menace in flood time. In places, between the Twisted Mountain on the east and the Jackfish Hills on the west, the river is a couple of miles wide, reckoning from the outermost snyes or back channels. The centre channel is high, and from it run offshoots to the side channels, cut afresh every year in the shifting gravel. In 1927 my partner, C.G. Matthews, and I started with a 4-h.p. Johnson outboard. This we smashed on a snag in the calm water at the outset, so we reverted once more to the primitive, and relayed a heavy outfit in sections up to Deadmen's Valley. By the time that job was done there were few shortcuts in the Splits that I had not tested at one stage of water or another. Odd memories come of those trips—moose and bears swimming the channels—the time the bald-headed eagle took a dive at us—duck shooting as we ran downstream.

Facing page, top: Albert Faille's cabin. Facing page, bottom: Gordon Matthews, 1927.

And one trip in February 1929 when, snowshoeing down through the Splits in a cold spell and carrying only one light blanket, I camped on a wooded island. It was very cold—over 50 degrees below, I found later from Jack La Flair—and I decided to improve on the previous night's camp. Long ago I had read a yarn of Jack London's about some trip on the Yukon. The hero of this yarn made his camps with the smooth precision of a machine, and must be an example to follow. Anyway, I would try one of his tricks and see how it went.

While I was fixing up camp I made two fires on ground that I had cleared of snow. When the wood and spruce boughs were cut and the chores done, I swept one fire into the other and made my bed in the warm ashes. The black, jagged Jackfish Mountains knifed up in the west into the green afterglow of a cold-weather sunset. The ice of the many channels, and even the trees, provided a fusillade from a phantom army. Camp looked snug.

But there was something wrong with that fellow's idea—or something lacking in the way I had carried it out. The heat drew the damp out of the ground into my spruce boughs and blanket. Then it all froze again, and so did I—above and below—and if I hadn't packed a furnace inside me, I'd be there watching the Jackfish Mountains to this day. I never tried it again.

The river, always fast, draws together really as you pass through some foothill ridges, and ahead lies the plateau of the First Canyon—about 12 or 13 miles through. At the gateway into the canyon, on the right bank and some hundreds of yards back from the Nahanni, are the famous hot springs. They flow, in separate streams, each of a different temperature, from the foot of a cliff across a small, grassy meadow, reaching the river in one creek, which warms the Nahanni, down that bank, for a couple of hundred yards. It seems a shame to spoil a good yarn, but, in cold weather it is just as cold alongside these springs as it is on the canyon ice, and they, like others up the Liard and elsewhere, exercise just as much general effect on the climate as a hot bath would do, if stood outside, or a well-heated stock trough. There is no tropical valley.

To lie in one of the streamlets on a May day, in the sunshine, with the hot water flowing over you, is a joy. And the springs sub-irrigate and warm their little patch of meadow, so that, as early as mid-May, there is green grass showing and violets are in bloom there.

Some of the finest scenery on the Nahanni is in this First or Lower Canyon. The water is fast and the riffles strong, and the great, green river drives under cliffs that rise almost sheer 1,500 feet and then, with a slope of talus intervening, on up to 3,000 feet. Matthews and I ran down through that canyon one sunny morning after rain. "We slid between the great cliffs," my diary reads, "and down riffle after riffle, hardly talking, sometimes a long way apart, watching the green, grey and purple of the canyon sides, with the soft clouds moving along them and pouring down the gullies."

Those heights are no guesswork. Held up by high water, I climbed up the cleft of a creek in the canyon with an aneroid in my pocket. As the cliffs levelled off I went on, and (I quote again from my diary) "at 4,000 feet I came out into a wonderful country . . . the open pastures of the caribou and the mountain sheep . . . miles and miles of high, close cropped grazing lands . . . At last I perched on a rock on the top of a round grass hill at a height of 4,500 feet above the Nahanni. The whole green, flower-starred upland lay around me, with the sunlight, and the rainstorms, and a cold wind sweeping over it. It was rent into a maze of canyons and deep valleys, out of which came the noise of water and the boiling cloud vapours. I could see the country beyond the Liard, lazy in the sunshine, the Twisted Mountain, Nahanni Butte, fifty miles away." Those were high and never-to-be-forgotten days.

These alplands in wintertime provide feed for the Dall sheep and a highway for the Nahannis, who spend most of the summer around South Nahanni, in the surrounding hill country, or going down to Fort Simpson for treaty. After freeze-up they set out with their dog teams for the Upper Nahanni or the country of the Yukon Territory Divide—following the river ice where it suits them to do so, or striking across country above timberline direct to their hunting grounds, avoiding the windings of the river and the canyons, bare of game in wintertime. The range to the southwest of Deadmen's Valley they call the Tlogo-Tsho—the Big Prairie Mountains—and through this range, by the Meilleur River, they have a trail to the Beaver River in the Yukon. There and elsewhere in that upper country, they hunt till spring, sending perhaps a party in to the post at Eastertime. In the springtime, skin boats are made and the hunters come in down the Nahanni or down the Beaver River, with their catch of fur, hunting beaver on the way.

There is good reason for avoiding the Nahanni canyons, whenever possible, in wintertime. In places they freeze late

Facing page: The dogs at Patterson and Matthews's cabin on the Nahanni, 1928.

and, even in February, there are stretches of open water and much overflow. Ledges of ice sometimes run along under the canyon walls and peter out to nothing, becoming so narrow that a man who has ventured too far with a dog team may have difficulty in turning back. One of these places, in the Lower Canyon, we crossed on Christmas Day, 1928, with a canoe—dogs, sled and everything. A squall of wind came howling down the canyon. The dogs, helpful as always when afloat, crowded all to the lee side and over we went. Luckily there was some birchbark and a big driftpile handy—the grub box had headed on downstream—so, if we had no Christmas dinner, at least the canyon was illuminated that night. A fire like an Armada beacon made the shadows dance on a thousand feet of cliff, and thawed and warmed the sodden voyageurs.

At the head of the Lower Canyon sits the Cache Rapid—a sort of entrance fee to Deadmen's Valley, which lies beyond.

In this valley, 40 years ago, the two half-breed McLeods were found killed—tied to trees, so the story goes, and headless. They had come out the year before, bringing with them coarse gold from somewhere in that vast country—perhaps from the Flat River. They went back in, accompanied by a white man, the following year, and disappeared. Eventually, their remains were found near the head of Deadmen's Valley in the spruce on the left bank of the Nahanni, and perhaps a couple of miles below the entrance to the Second Canyon. The white man was never seen again.

That, and the killing of Jorgenson, gave the Nahanni a bad name. Jorgenson's cabin was on the Nahanni, opposite the mouth of Flat River, on a flat now washed out by the high waters. He had been walking from the cabin to the river, with a couple of buckets, for water. Suddenly he must have seen something that scared him, for he dropped the buckets and ran for the cabin to get his rifle. The bullet overtook him as he ran—and there he was found, face downwards, between the river and the shack, which was burned. It was believed he had found gold up the Flat.

That is the story as it was given to me and this, coupled with the affair of the McLeods, and with the various other disappearances in that wild country, put a devil-devil on the deep, swift-running river that caused men to speak of it with respect.

There were also the half-mythical Mountain Men— wandering Indians of the Mackenzie Mountains and the Yukon Divide. I know for certain that, as late as the early 1930s, Indians from Wrigley, where Matthews was trading then, would not go away back into those western fastnesses. Bad men, they said, the Mountain Men were, trading in to no post, keeping their country to themselves, bad medicine to strangers. All I can add to this story is that, in August 1927, Faille and I saw, near the mouth of the Flat River, two fresh and unexplained blazes. The chips were fresh—and we were, so far as we knew, the only men from the Liard country on the South Nahanni.

Away up above the Falls, and then up the Rabbit Kettle River, lie the Snyder Mountains, a geologically new range of pinnacles, sheer precipices and great snow- and icefields from which the Nahanni draws its volume and its power. In those mountains, Colonel H.M. Snyder and his guide, Jim Ross, were stalked by a grizzly in broad daylight. The Colonel saw it and shouted to Ross, and the grizzly's head now hangs on the wall at the 7s Ranch on the Red Deer River. Any country where a man is such a rarity that a grizzly will try to lunch off him under the noonday sun is a lonely and an empty land. And they saw no axe cuts in that part of the Nahanni area. The Indians evidently give those mountains a wide berth, and, in country like this and over such a great area, what can be more natural than that occasionally a man, travelling alone, should disappear? A slip, the snagging of a trackline, a squall of wind in the canyon or, apparently, even a hungry grizzly—and another notch is added to the Nahanni's tally.

Matthews and I built our cabin in the centre of Deadmen's Valley and wintered there in 1928–29. Since "tropical valleys" are news now and then, a resume of that winter there may be of interest. The river froze over in late October, pretty solidly. Then the Chinooks started—and what Chinooks! They blew all day in the valley and at night they would retreat up onto the tops of the Tlogo-Tsho. You could hear the southwest wind howling up there in the darkness—and about 10 A.M. the first warm breeze would come stealing across the flats, back down again for another day's work. They licked up all the snow, broke up the river and piled the ice up on the beaches. To people who wanted to trap, haul home moosemeat and get around easily, they were a perfect curse. On and off they blew till Christmas Eve, and then (as nothing ever comes in moderation on the Nahanni) they stopped—quite suddenly and completely. The next Chinook was March 11th and, in between, there was no depth of cold, no violence of storm, that was not well and truly sampled. Late in April and early in May, on warm sunny days, came the big, bumbling mosquitoes, the sweet smell of the poplar buds and the sound of running water. The ice went out early in May, and on May 12th Starke and Stevens appeared with their scow at our camp. They had run down through the canyons from Caribou Creek on the Flat River, where the winter had been quite different from ours—much less windy in cold weather, the snow not very deep, and no unseasonable Chinooks.

Facing page: Colonel H.M. Snyder at his hunting lodge, Sundre, Alberta.

Re-reading an old diary brings back memories of that camp in Deadmen's Valley—of moose on the bars in the summertime, the white sheep on the hills, and of seven black bears and a grizzly in one vast berry patch at one and the same time. And of the winter days when the game was gone—to the Yukon, to some sunnier, more open range—and you couldn't find a steak on four legs in all the valley.

Of the shooting of a wolf at timberline under the spurs of the Tlogo-Tsho, when the rifle flashes split through the dusk of an October evening—and of a far-off timberline camp up on a fork of Ram Creek, a place of unimaginable loneliness. Here, great boulders, the size of cabins, lay piled in wild confusion, and over them grew moss so thick that it covered them as with a carpet. Stunted, wind-twisted trees grew in this moss, and a man with a pack could travel over it—and occasionally put his foot clean through it into empty space beneath. Dangerous going . . .

And so onwards from the valley and through the Second Canyon—massive walls and more sheer, but easier water than the Lower Canyon—and into the Little Valley, another triangular opening in the mountains, but much smaller than Deadmen's Valley.

The Third Canyon reaches from here nearly to the Flat River, which must be about a hundred miles from Nahanni Butte by water. This canyon has everything—bad water and good, cliffs that tower over 4,000 feet above the river, a box canyon that can be a problem in canoeing, and that magnificent piece of rock scenery, the Gate. The country is more broken, sheep and bears are to be met with along this stretch of river until, some 12 miles above the Gate, the canyon walls recede and the Nahanni is flanked from here to the Falls canyon by an intricate, tangled hill country.

Facing page, top: Patterson and Matthews's cabin.

Facing page, bottom: Part of the interior of the cabin.

The Flat River, with its clear green water, drains down from the Yukon Territory Divide and the southwest slopes

of the Snyder Mountains, to enter the Nahanni nine or ten miles above the Third Canyon. The Indians call it Too Naga, the Wolverine Water, and, with Caribou Creek, it drains a vast country, somewhere in which may lie the gold that so many have sought. The Indian camps that I saw in the first 75 miles of this river were all old, but a trail is said to run into its headwaters from Frances Lake in the Yukon.

The Flat River is a story to itself, but one sight of it, in September of 1928, is worth recording from my diary. "After a sudden sharp night frost . . . I saw the mountain tops next morning completely scarlet against the deep blue sky, all the way from Caribou to Irvine Creek. It was an unforgettable picture—the eye, travelling upwards from the emerald green water of the river, took in every shade of green and gold, to run out at timberline on to an even line of rounded mountain tops, each one standing out against the sky completely and dramatically scarlet."

A few miles before the traveller up the Nahanni reaches the Flat, a new thing becomes apparent—when you lay your ear to the pillow at night you can feel in the ground the vibration of the great waterfall. Yet from the camp where I first noticed this, to the falls, must be 16 air miles. Then again one can hear their actual sound plainly from a certain spot up the Flat River, which cannot be less than ten air miles away, with hills in between. The spray from them, at night, will drift a mile down the Nahanni, round the bend into the next reach, and fill with water the hollows in the cover of your sleeping bag.

Some of the worst water on the lower Nahanni is between the mouth of the Flat River and the Falls, but when the last bend is rounded—what a sight to see! I drifted in my canoe in the pool below the Falls, on an Facing page: The Gate of August day of 1927, and marvelled at that the Nahanni. magnificent cataract, its creaming rim set against a deep blue sky. This, then, was the thunder that had sounded in the earth so many miles away—this plunge of the Nahanni from the rock islet where the water first quickens, down in two great leaps, splitting on the lower step against a large pyramid of rock—a drop of 316 feet from the islet to the pool.

The spray from the Falls brought a coolness into that blazing afternoon. Almost, it seemed that they were getting closer . . .

Suddenly I came back to earth and let drive with the paddle. I had passed over the dead-water point and was being drawn downhill in the backlash toward the falls. A few seconds more and it would have been too late; as it was, I had to make a frantic dig for it. Slowly, very slowly, I drew in to the foot of the portage trail and the safety of dry land.

20 Those Earlier Hills

All good things come to an end, and there came a day when we turned our canoes down the Liard and saw Nahanni Butte sink below the horizon—perhaps for the last time? Then it was that I realized we had been allowed to live for a little time in a world apart: a lonely world, of surpassing beauty, that had given us all things from the sombre magnificence of the canyons to the gay sunshine of those windswept uplands; from the utter silence of the dry side canyons to the uproar of the broken waters; land where men pass, and the silence falls back into place behind them—The Land of Shadows. 🔲

Facing page: The Gate, with Pulpit Rock. Note Faille heading downriver in his canoe.

The Nahany Lands

The Beaver, Summer 1961

A letter was written by Governor Simpson at Fort Chipewyan on January 2nd, 1823. The letter was to Chief Trader A.R. McLeod of Mackenzie's River Forks at the Junction of the Liard (soon to be called Fort Simpson), and in it the Governor said that he was sending down a new clerk, J.M. McLeod, to supersede Charles Brisbois. He went on to say that the country in general was becoming depleted in fur ". . . and if we expect to make profits we must extend the Trade to Countries, hitherto unexplored." The Governor was particularly anxious that a communication should be opened with the Nahanis, adding, "I trust you will set every engine to work consistent with your means."

A.R. McLeod evidently lost no time but set out there and then up the Liard to the South Nahanni—which was known then as the Nahany River or the North Branch of Rivière au Liard. The report of that winter journey is missing but there is an entry in the fort journal for March 6th: "Mr. Alex R. Macleod returned from his Journey of discovery—which did not terminate agreeable to his wishes . . . Mr. Macleod suffered considerably from privation—for the natives who accompanied him were no animal Hunters."

Facing page: The Falls of the Nahanni.

McLeod did find, however, that there was plenty of beaver in the part of the Nahanni country that he visited: ". . . and that the Country also abounds in Animals for the natives to make great quantities of Provisions." It would seem that he did not make contact with the Nahanis, who preferred to remain hidden in their mountains—in his opinion, through fear of the hostile Indians of Fort Liard. Early in April he wrote to the Governor that, previous efforts having failed, he had "appointed Mr. John McLeod to command a party . . . on a voyage of discovery to the Westward."

The fair copies, in his own handwriting, of J.M. McLeod's journals of his two Nahanni explorations are preserved in the Hudson's Bay Company's Archives. The 1823 report is headed: "Occurrences of a Voyage to the Nahany Lands."

McLeod left Mackenzie's River Forks at 9:00 A.M. on June 5th in a north canoe. His crew consisted of two Canadians, one half-breed as interpreter and seven Indians. The Liard River was in flood, the going was tough, and at 8:00 P.M. they made camp "in sight of the pine Island at the foot of the Rapids." McLeod ended the first day's struggle against the current with a glass of rum to his men and "a small quantity of very weak stuff to the Indians."

These people were accustomed to making early starts. However, with a crew consisting mostly of Indians, it was useless to insist on the usual travelling hours of the Canadian voyageur and in consequence, the party did not hit the river till the late hour of 4:30 A.M. They came to the foot of the rapids at 6:00 and there they took to the trackline, continuing with the line all day and camping at 8:30 P.M. a little below Cape Island.

Facing page: A canoe being tracked.

At noon on the following day they came to an Indian camp where, to McLeod's regret, he was obliged to remain for the rest

of that day and all the next, outfitting and hiring Indians for the trip and gumming his canoe. Unfortunately, the number of Indians hired is not given. It would have been interesting to know, in view of the amount of game the party killed and consumed.

They started again on the 9th, three Indians being sent ahead in two small canoes to hunt, and the big canoe leaving at 8:00 A.M. Four more Indians joined them on that day as they surged up the Long Reach toward the mountains with the help of a following wind and a blanket sail. This probably brought the party up to at least 20 men—possibly more. This seems a large number, but they were going into an unknown country to look for a band of Indians who might be anywhere in that tumbled wilderness of mountains. The methods they used made numbers essential: they fanned out to hunt, to light signal fires above timberline or along the Nahanni River, to look for tracks or signs of Nahani camps. They would reunite late in the evening—or sometimes, even, days later—heading for the smoke of the main party's fire. And with the Nahanis an unknown quantity there would have been an added confidence in the presence of a large and well-armed party.

Early in the afternoon of June 10th they turned into the mouth of the Nahanni and at 6:00 they made camp about five miles up that river. The 110 miles up the Liard River in flood had been dealt with in a fraction over four days' travelling time. Into camp, after dark, came the hunters who had gone ahead in the light canoes; they brought in a black bear and a beaver. Other hunters had been dropped off on the Liard to cross the Nahanni Range on foot "in search of Mountain Goat." There are no goat in those parts: that is the name that McLeod uses almost throughout his diary for the *ovis dalli*, the wild white sheep of the Mackenzie Mountains. It was the meat of one of these that the hunters brought into camp the next morning.

Oppressed by thunder and a downpour that lasted all day, they started up the Nahanni—which was high and rising. Soon an Indian shot a bull moose and that was dealt with in the rain. Then they came to the end of the calm water and the desolation of the Splits faced them—driftpiles and shingle bars, a driving current, whirlpools at the foot of dangerous, undercut banks. "The Courses of this river is very various, and the Channels much obstructed by shoals and drift wood." The Nahanni was rising fast, and so a little was enough of the Splits in flood-time; they could do better on foot on dry land, and at 4:00 P.M. they landed to camp and cache the canoe. They stayed in that camp two nights, owing to the torrential rain, and they built a platform on which to lay up the big canoe, lashing it there with the trackline. That camp was on the southwest side of the Nahanni, below the mouth of Mattson Creek.

From there, delayed at intervals by the frightful weather of the rainy season and by bad going, they struck "inland"—that is, away from the Nahanni. McLeod counts his progress by the number of ranges crossed "west of the river." A range, with him, is not necessarily what a geographer would call a mountain range: it can be anything from a mountain ridge to a true range. Once that has been appreciated, and by taking note of every small clue, McLeod's "ranges" can be sorted out and his general course established. Few landmarks are described: the diary is a record of hours travelled, the general direction, weather, events, and the game that was killed.

By the time the party had crossed the first range they were practically out of the provisions they had brought from the Forks, having had to share these with the Indians: from then onwards they depended on their guns. The hunters promised McLeod "mountain goat" about a day's march farther on and he was in no way worried. Two days from there brought them to the banks of the Jackfish River, which separates McLeod's third and fourth ranges; they were probably about 16 miles up from the Nahanni. "In this river there is a sufficiency of water for North Canoes, but as far as the view could extend nothing but a constant chain of Rapids appeared to the sight." McLeod's Indians told him that where this river joined the Nahanni they usually made pine-bark canoes to run down to the Liard. As the party travelled they fired a number of driftpiles along the Jackfish River, "on the West side of which we encamped." The smoke of these fires, it was hoped, would be a signal to any wandering Nahanis.

Late on June 17th they gained the summit of the fifth range, by which McLeod must mean the northeastern escarpment of the Tlogo-Tsho Mountains south of Deadmen's Valley. They travelled above timberline and camped up there: wood was scarce and a little snow came down; the first caribou appeared. The name "Tlogo-Tsho" means "Big Prairie" and refers to the grassy, alpine country on those level summits above timberline. Seen from the air those mountains are still open and free of scrub or timber. They were probably even more open in McLeod's time since he was travelling at the coldest point of what climatologists call "The Little Ice Age." It was a time of extended glaciation and maximum rain and cold, and timberline was low.

There has been a warming up since then, accelerated since 1900 and greatly accelerated since 1920. This has produced plainly visible results in the area of McLeod's travels. In Deadmen's Valley, for example, timberline is climbing fast, so that what was open moorland country in 1928—just beneath the escarpment of the Tlogo-Tsho—is today a jungle of willow and alder and small trees. Travelling and hunting are infinitely more difficult and this change in timberline, which must be widespread, has probably affected adversely the sheep and the caribou. Changes of this nature, added to the fact that McLeod makes no reference to the magnetic variation (though he may have been instructed in this by W.F. Wentzel who was then at Mackenzie's Forks and understood something of these matters) make it difficult to plot the expedition's trail in detail beyond the fifth range.

They marched onwards in a northwesterly direction, above

timberline where that was possible, sometimes going hungry, sometimes feasting on sheep and caribou. They came to the Meilleur River, which flows down to Deadmen's Valley, and they crossed it and its tributary streams. (I am using the modern names, for McLeod named nothing.) Beyond the sixth range they found an early spring camp of the Nahanis and beyond the seventh range they came on an old winter camp. At this point the party was out of meat completely and some of the Indians and the interpreter were losing heart. McLeod, however, was determined to go on. The game seemed to have vanished and in three days they only got one cow caribou. They swung to the southwest for a day; then for two days they headed back southeast, then west to the ninth range where they ran into caribou once more and ate their fill. All this time they were making fires on high summits, looking for tracks, watching for distant smokes.

They camped west of the ninth range for several days. The Indians were sent out in various directions, and on June 27th McLeod and the interpreter climbed a mountain north of camp. They got a fine view and McLeod writes: "To the Westward I could perceive no regular ranges of mountains, altho' some parts appeared very high but much broken and detached, the valleys appeared well wooded." That description fits in exactly with the plateau type of country toward the heads of the Meilleur River and over the Yukon Territory boundary to the Beaver River— today a country of small forest, a vast number of beaver dams, and mountains rising above timberline in isolated masses of barren rock.

This camp was McLeod's farthest into the Nahani country

in either year: it was probably north of the Meilleur, for some of the Indians, returning to camp from a westerly exploration of two days' duration, reported that they "fell on a River which they suppose to be the Nahany River," the current of which was swift and the banks well wooded. This was probably Caribou Creek, a tributary of the Flat River, and so of the Nahanni. On his way down the mountain that evening McLeod shot three caribou. He was now convinced that the Nahanis were somewhere between this ninth range camp and the Liard.

They broke camp the next day and headed southeast. Four long days saw them back on the summit of the fourth range, marching above timberline toward the Nahanni River—and there, crossing the range in a southerly direction, they came on fresh tracks of the Nahanis. They turned and followed them, down into the valley of the Jackfish River, continuing in pursuit till 9:30 P.M.

They were on the trail again at 2:30 A.M., following up the Jackfish River. Suddenly the tracks turned aside and climbed the fourth range again. McLeod's party followed and "had some difficulty in obtaining the Summit. Still the Nahany Indians make no scruple in climbing up precipices with their Women and Children, where none of my men, and very few of the Indians would venture." On reaching the summit they saw a smoke at a distance and answered it. They went on, and soon ". . . both parties approached each other very slowly. Yelling, Singing and Dancing as they advanced, at 7 P.M. Both partys joined unarmed, each holding a small piece of meat in their hand—shortly after a Dance was formed,

Facing page: The Flat River, a major tributary of the Nahanni.

which amusement continued for the remainder of the day." The strange Indians were 14 in number, mostly of medium size, good figure and fresh complexion. Their language was "fluent and harmonious, but they vociferate it out with such incredible force, that it is on the whole disagreeable." Two of McLeod's Indians, who had been sent out on a reconnaissance on June 30th, were found with the Nahanis. This may have helped in bringing about this amicable first meeting with the Company's men on July 3rd, 1823.

The next day opened with the giving of presents. To the "Nahany Leader" a chief's coat and various finery: a "Half Ax, Hand Dag. Knife, Looking Glass, Small Kittle and a small piece of Red Oriell feathers—which articles he seemed to be highly satisfied." To the rest other presents were given, including firesteels and vermilion. McLeod accepted a present "of Seventeen Martins" and allowed his own Indians to trade what furs the Nahanis had—"a few Martins, some Beavers, Cats and a Bear Skin or two." McLeod urged the leader to show his trade goods to all his people. He arranged a rendezvous and signals for the following year and said he would be back with a good stock of useful articles to trade for fur.

"The Nahanys," McLeod writes, "appear to be a manly race of men and good hunters, they are smart, active and quick in their motions, and are not haughty, but seem to be peaceably inclined without the appearance of fears or meanness. They are Cleanly, Hospitable and Sociable. The (White Eyes) Leader . . . is a tall strong and robust built man." He was bearded, which gave him the "looks of an old Roman Sage." From him McLeod obtained various information on the country and the tribes to the westward—eliciting the fact that most of this Nahani tribe inhabited the Upper Liard country, and that it was three winters since the chief had visited them. Toward evening the Nahanis drew off to join their families. Some of McLeod's men went with them and the night in the Nahani camp was passed in singing and dancing.

On July 5th McLeod started for home. That evening, shortly before camping time, an Indian killed six sheep and the party proceeded on its homeward way well provided with meat, arriving at Mackenzie's Forks at 8:00 A.M. on July 10th. On this 1823 trip McLeod and his hunters had killed 35 head of large animals—22 caribou, 9 sheep, 3 moose and a bear—besides a few odds and ends.

The Second Trip

The date of departure was June 8th, 1824. "I left Fort Simpson Forks McKenzie's River in a North Canoe. My Crew consisted of one Canadian and two Half-breeds Engages with Two Indians." Three Indians joined the party on the way up the Liard, making a total strength of nine. The current was stronger and the water higher than in 1823, and a new hazard was added in the wide canyon of the Lower Rapids: "the quantity of ice . . . along the Banks of the River made the tracking very bad and in several places the Men's lives were endangered by pieces falling down." They arrived at the Nahanni mouth at 2:00 P.M. on June 12th, having—as before—dropped off two Indians to cross the range "in search of Mountain Goats." They camped near the foot of Nahanni Butte and signal fires were lighted on the summit of that mountain. The famous mosquitoes of South

Nahanni were on the warpath as usual: "Weather very Warm and Musquitoes worse and worse." In the night the Nahanni rose over three feet and reached the canoe and gear, carrying away some of the paddles.

They went on into the Splits, firing driftpiles on the islands. Against the June flood they "proceeded with very little progress." Eventually they swung over into the snyes, or back channels, of the southwest shore and went on until they found a good place for laying up the canoe, some distance below the mouth of the Jackfish River. A "Moose Deer and two Otters" obligingly presented themselves right in camp in a downpour of rain.

At noon on June 15th they started up the Jackfish River and that evening they camped on top of the fourth range, making signal fires but receiving no answering smoke. On the next day they sighted at a distance the Nahanni River below the Lower Canyon. It was there that McLeod had made a rendezvous with Indians from Willow Lake, a large lake east of the Mackenzie Mountains. But there was no sign of them so they went on, passing south of the canyon uplands and well back from the river. One Indian was detached to hunt sheep and two more to follow the river as nearly as they could and send up smokes.

The afternoon of June 18th found the party on the uplands of Deadmen's Valley. They could see the Nahanni in the distance, at a place where it was calm and slow, and where, the Indians said, they sometimes crossed on rafts. That quiet stretch of water is at the mouth of Ram Creek at the lower end of Deadmen's Valley. The Indians told McLeod that at some distance below the quiet water it was not practicable for any craft to pass—"and in My own opinion as far as I could see with my Glass, I think it not practicable in the present state of the Water, the Mountain through which the bed of the River flows being perpendicular on both sides." They were looking at the upper entrance to the Lower Canyon of the Nahanni.

Camp was high up in the valley, close under the spurs of the Tlogo-Tsho. Sheep and moose were in sight and they shot one of each. The mosquitoes were "as thick as the dust that flies before the Wind." Far away, beyond the mountains to the north, a smoke rose in the sky. That, they thought, could only be from the Willow Lakers, who should have met them by the river. The five Indians with McLeod now declared their fear of going in search of the Nahanis with so small a party. McLeod, as a compromise, agreed to wait in that camp till June 23rd; then, even if the Willow Lakers had not yet joined them, he would go on, alone with his men if need be. So they camped, climbing and setting their fires, hunting and gorging themselves (they shot one more moose and nine sheep), and part-drying the meat they were to carry. And on the 22nd it snowed.

On that day two Indians went to the summit of the Bald Mountain. Away in the southwest, between the fifth range (which they were on) and the seventh range they thought they could see a smoke. That was enough for McLeod and he broke camp early on June 23rd. The Indians "remonstrated for some time, but seeing that I was determined on going, they began to arrange their little bundles to follow." Toward evening, between the fifth and sixth ranges, an Indian shot two sheep. That ended the day's travel. "According to Indian custom we put up for the Night at 8 P.M.—Where all hands before a blazing fire passed a Night of festivity upon excellent Venison."

The first encounter with the Nahanis was with an isolated hunter—then with a group of four. These were given presents, each one, of knives, and one was sent ahead to inform White Eyes of McLeod's approach. The two parties met on the afternoon of June 25th, on one of the tributary streams of the Meilleur River, between the sixth and seventh ranges. The Nahanis were pleased to see McLeod and said they had been on their way to the rendezvous. McLeod was disappointed to find they had made no hunts worth mentioning but for this they blamed privation and the severity of the winter. Questions to the leader as to the Nahani country produced little result for want of a good interpreter. McLeod then proposed to the leader to accompany him "to the Southward of the Mountains" where he hoped to find Chief Trader Murdoch McPherson and a party of Fort Liard Indians. This camp on the Meilleur was close to headwaters of the Beaver River in the Yukon Territory where McPherson was carrying out an exploration. But White Eyes would have nothing of this suggestion, nor would he let any of his people put themselves within reach of the Fort Liard Indians. However, McLeod finally prevailed on him to come with two of his family to Fort Simpson. Singing and dancing and the giving of presents rounded off the day.

The Nahanis accompanied McLeod on his homeward trail as far as the summit of the fifth range, the plan being that McLeod's party would shoot meat for all before they parted company. That splendid hunting ground of the Tlogo-Tsho did not fail them: McLeod spotted a herd of caribou with his glass, and his Indians and the Nahanis were sent to surround them: in less than two hours they had nine. McLeod's men took a small amount of the meat and then, after the most touching farewells between the Nahanis, they went on their way, accompanied by White Eyes, his son and his nephew.

Second thoughts speedily overcame the Nahani leader. He awoke next morning troubled with bad dreams and wished to return. McLeod reasoned with him: "assured him that his dreams would turn out quite the reverse of what he then anticipated, after some time had elapsed in Interpreting the Old Leader's dreams, with some fine words and few promises, he with some reluctance agreed to follow, and was under way at 5:00 A.M."

The rest of the journey back to the canoe was misery itself. On the afternoon of June 28th they were caught on top of the fourth range by thunder and lightning and a blinding whirl of snow. They were forced to camp there for the rest of the day and through the night—a most wretched camp, seeking shelter "among the Crevices of the Rocks from the inclemency of the Weather, having no wood to make a fire."

Almost all of the next day they travelled along the crest of the range, coming down to the Jackfish River at 7:00 P.M. They saw plenty of sheep but could not get at them; they went supperless to bed. "Rain and thick mist. Course: E." The last day was almost the worst. They started, empty and hungry, at 4:00 A.M. and at 7:00 P.M. they came to the Nahanni. The old chief was tired and wished to camp but there was nothing to eat, only the pemmican cached with the canoe to hope for, so he was induced to "trudge on." The Nahanni had risen much, making the going "Misserable bad" and it took them four more hours to reach the canoe. Misfortune still had in store one parting kick; the pemmican had been "eaten by the small Animals (supposed

Martins)." With what feelings they fell asleep we are not told.

In the morning the Nahanis examined the canoe minutely and greatly admired it, being particularly taken with the lightness of "such a Large Vehicle." Several hours were spent in gumming and arranging the canoe, "and only was ready to throw in the Water at 1 P.M." They embarked—and the Nahani leader, finding himself afloat on the racing floodwaters was at first much afraid, this being the first occasion for himself or any of his people to travel by canoe. They reached the Liard at 5:00 P.M. and, since the night was fine, they drifted on downstream without stopping, sleeping by turns and as best they could, and arriving at Fort Simpson at 2:00 P.M. the following day.

Shortly before arrival the Nahanis again became worried and fearful. They were calmed by McLeod, "altho' for some time after entering the House, they seemed lost in astonishment and surprise."

That is the end of McLeod's second report. One might add that on this trip 34 large animals were killed and recorded—16 caribou, 15 sheep and 3 moose. Good manners forbade any interrogation of White Eyes on the day of arrival but on the following day, July 3rd, a proper parley was held through an interpreter. The language seemed to Wentzel, who recorded the results in the fort journal, "to be much the same as the Fort de Liard Indians, and has a strong affinity to the Beaver Indians of Peace River."

To summarize, the country was described: a plateau, well wooded and with isolated mountains, abounding in game and in beaver and the other fur-bearing animals. There were good fishing lakes, but the Nahanis were mountain Indians; they did not use canoes, nor did they make nets or secure a living from fishing.

The Nahanis agreed to bring good hunts to Fort Simpson in the spring of 1826, coming on the crust of the snow. They would not consider going to Fort Liard; they were in dread of the Fort Liard Indians with whom they were at war—which was why they kept concealed in their mountains. The only other Indians they knew were the Dahadinnis who were many and who held all the country west of the mountains from the source of the Nahanni to the sea, where white men traded with those that were nearest to the sea—"Does not know what sea, points however to the westward."

The leader refused to draw a map of his country. The Nahanis made a small trade and were advised as to the proper dressing of skins. "Music seems to delight them and in short they were lost in wonder and admiration."

The leader spoke at the end. "I am like a Child now in my own estimation, you treat us so well. That I have nothing to give makes me ashamed to speak, which is the reason I appear silent . . . all my Party and Children will be curious to come here and see what I have seen, it is the Whites who have made the Earth, we see that now."

On Sunday, July 4th, a new boat was launched and, in a high wind, McLeod sailed these wild men of the mountains over to the west shore of the Liard to start them on the long road home. They departed with their trade, 44 pounds of provisions and some presents—"pleased and elated beyond description."

South Nahanni Revisited

The Beaver, June 1952

To the north the rocky spurs of the Mackenzie Mountains came down to the river, white and cold-looking in the moonlight. To the south lay the low, forested banks that proclaimed the flat lands stretching back toward the far-off Alberta Plateau. Overhead a great September moon fought a losing battle with a magnificent aurora that streamed and spilled across the sky and put the stars to shame. Every colour of the rainbow was in it, and they in turn were reflected in the calm waters of the great river. The moon was down below there, too, and so were the golden poplars that lined the banks and crowded on the bars and islands—and, behind us, all this glory was split by our wake into a million pieces of gold and silver.

And I lay there, rolled in my eiderdown on the foredeck of the scow, listening to the rush of the Liard current beneath me and marvelling at all this beauty: no man, surely, ever had a more splendid bedground. And that was nothing but a piece of pure luck. We had spent eight weeks up the South Nahanni River and had figured on working south by canoe, 300 miles up the Liard and Fort Nelson rivers, back to the Alaska Road— and what should we do but fall in with Ed Cooper, up from the Mackenzie, in a hurry to get to Fort Nelson, driving his boat and scow night and day in the full of the moon! Just a piece of wonderful luck, and not the first we had

Facing page: A canoe being poled.

had by a long sight. Curtis always claimed our good fortune as his own private contribution to the outfit. "The Lord looks after Curtis," he would say, when a thunderstorm had just missed us or when, descending a loose scree, we had incautiously loosed off a ton or two of rock into the valley below. "The Lord always takes care of Curtis—and you two are with me, so why worry?" It was his outfit—Curtis R. Smith of St. Albans, Vermont. His friend Frank C. Wood was with him, and Curtis had invited me to make a third.

There was probably something in what he said about luck, for it had been a good summer. We had dropped down to Nahanni Butte from Fort Nelson in July, the three of us with two canoes. Then up to the Falls of the Nahanni, making a quick trip with Fred Sibbeston in his power boat, and caching our light canoe in Deadmen's Valley en route. From the Falls we ran down to the mouth of the Flat River, said goodbye to Fred, and then, with pole, line and paddle, struggled our 18-foot freight canoe some 75 river miles up the Flat to the mouth of Irvine Creek. There we had cached our outfit and made a sashay on foot westward, over a notch in a mountain barrier and on toward a jagged range of granite peaks that thrust up into the sunset out of the blue immensity of the caribou uplands. Late in August, when the first golden leaves were coming on the little poplars, we had come again to the cache and loaded up and turned the canoe's nose downstream—down many a riffle, through the Gate of the Nahanni and through the upper canyons, down to Deadmen's Valley, camping and climbing where and when we pleased.

Facing page: The Gate of the Nahanni, looking upstream.

There were so many memories—the sudden rush of white water in the riffles, the bobbing heads of swimming caribou, the swirl and struggle of the Arctic grayling and those gigantic Dolly Vardens of the Flat River. We had felt the steel-blue chill of evening in the canyons, and we had seen the golden glow of the morning sun breaking through the mists and lighting pinnacle after glowing pinnacle on 3,000 feet of canyon wall. And, returning to camp at dusk, we had seen the fire twinkling down below there, on the beaches, with its trail of blue woodsmoke drifting out onto the river. Comfortably weary and very hungry, how one blessed the fellow that had got home first!

And still there had been Deadmen's Valley and its queer side canyons to explore, and the swift rush down the Cache Rapid into the Lower Canyon, and so on down by the Hot Springs and the Twisted Mountain, through the fast channels of the Splits, until in the end we had come to a landing in the quiet water by Nahanni Butte. Yes—decidedly a good summer, I thought, and the more I thought of it, the better it became. The human memory could well take for its motto that old one that many an ancient sundial bears: *Horas non numero nisi serenas*—"I count only the sunlit hours." Already those few days of rain and shadow were fading.

The rush of the water under the nose of the scow was making me drowsy—the golden days of summer were crowding back in force . . .

There was that July day at the Falls. We roared up the last reaches of the Falls canyon in the bright morning sunshine, passing within a few yards of a wolverine, which had just killed a rabbit by the water's edge. He started to pack the rabbit up the mountainside; then he turned and snarled at us and in so doing dropped his rabbit. Hastily he retrieved it and scrambled away into a stony coulee, out of sight among the rocks and scrub. We swept on round the last bend and there, at the far end of the Falls reach, was the great white thunder. We had the sun behind us and it was still early morning—a rainbow was tautly stretched across the face of the waterfall, and the whole reach glittered with the flying spray. One could come to this place 20 times and never see it so perfectly. I had been there twice before but never at this time of day nor at this stage of water—and never had I seen the rainbow.

The Falls reach is about half a mile long and the water is fast. Slowly, with both outboards running full blast, we made our way up to the portage landing—a rocky, inhospitable beach close under the falls. Above us the crest foamed white and sparkling against the summer sky; down below, in the darkly boiling waters of the pool, one could discern the hump of dead water caused by the upsurge from the depths—a sort of vertical eddy. It had vivid memories for me—and for a moment I was back in that hot August afternoon of 1927 when, drifting carelessly in a small canoe, I had passed over the centre of the hump and found myself being drawn down the forward slope toward the Falls . . . Instinctively I rammed forward with my right foot, bracing myself again for those hard driving paddle strokes of long ago—and then I saw Curtis gazing at me wonderingly, and Frank jumping ashore with the line.

We landed and walked up over the portage trail on the southwest bank to the calm water of the Upper Nahanni, climbing at least 500 feet before dropping down again to the river. Upstream from the head of the portage the river is like a lake, calm and placid. But, level with the upper landing, there is a small rock island, and below it the Nahanni rushes down a cataract, perhaps 500 yards in length and with a drop of at least 40 feet, to the lip of the first plunge. The fall itself—the largest in the Northwest Territories, with a drop of 316 feet—comes down in two steps with a rocky pyramid on the lower one that splits the final fall in two.

There you have the statistics. But we had also the deepest of blue skies, with snow-white thunderheads climbing into it over the barren-looking sheep mountains to the northeast. There were all the varied greens of the northern forest—and there was this wild water, blue and white, lashing and roaring down the cataract like some savage beast, to vanish over the lip of the Falls, clouding the dripping pyramid with spray, thundering into the pool below. And there was still the rainbow. Hanging with my left hand onto a dwarf fir, my feet insecurely planted in a mixture of moss and Labrador Tea, I reached out over the edge of the precipice with my camera strapped to my right hand. It was worth a little effort—not everybody has taken a picture of a rainbow from above. It was impossible to sight, so I pulled the trigger blind and hoped for the best. The result proved to be well worth the risk.

Facing page: The cataract above the Falls.

And there was Albert Faille, the last of the old-timers on the Nahanni. He and I had said goodbye 23 years ago at the Twisted Mountain, and now, in July of 1951, Faille was somewhere up here, the only man besides ourselves in all this wilderness of the Upper Nahanni. Not till we were 40 miles up the Flat River did

we come upon his sign. As we were eating our midday meal by the water's edge, a grizzly shuffled into view, working his way along the base of a cliff on the north side. He seemed interested in something in an eddy over there, but he saw us and decided that there were foreign devils in his bailiwick and scuffled away, with an annoyed "Woof!", up the mountainside. Later on we crossed over to investigate and found a great dead timber wolf, with a bullet hole in him, bobbing up and down in the clear water.

We found Faille camped by the great pool at Irvine Creek. "So you've come back," he said to me, as we shook hands, "after all these years!" A day went by as we fished, cooked, loafed—and talked. Several outsize fish came ashore, at Frank's invitation, to grace the table: one whale of a Dolly Varden had seven mice in him, laid neatly head to tail, and another contained six mice, one salamander and one small fish. What with Faille stimulating Frank's culinary genius to new and wilder ways of cooking trout, the place soon began to hum gently of baked fish and timber wolf.

For Faille had been in the wolf business. He had been up the Nahanni since October 1950 and had had scurvy for the first time in his life. Not recognizing the malady for what it was until his teeth began to get loose, he had become pretty weak by spring and early summer, and at that season the timber wolf, bringing the young out of the den to teach them to hunt, is interested in anything, including a weakened man. Unfortunately, from the wolves' point of view, they had picked the wrong man to demonstrate on: four great wolves lay dead, one on our side of the river, two on Faille's side, on the bar at the mouth of Irvine Creek, and one in the bush—and not one was over 200 yards from Faille's mosquito net: the closest 50 yards. Then there was that one in the eddy down the river, and two more that had dragged themselves away to die—seven in all, good shooting. We cremated one and dragged the rest into the river—brutes the size of Shetland ponies.

Facing page: The rocky pyramid that splits the Falls.

Faille was camped over the river from us in the big spruce. In 1928, when I had last seen it, the old carved tree was still standing. "Irvine Creek," it said, "July 1, 1921, A. F. E. Brown. Frank Rae," and below that "July 1 Rain. July 2 Rain. July 3 Rain. July 4 Rain." These two well-sprinkled travellers had made their way through the mountains from the Yukon, and it would be more than interesting to hear their story. Mr. Brown lives, I believe at Carcross, YT.

The old tree had fallen, and Faille had rolled it over and cut the blaze out to take it down to Fort Simpson—that fall, or sometime in 1952, it mattered little to him. Twice, at least, he had spent over two years on the Nahanni without seeing a living soul. We stood by the old blazed tree talking, Faille and I. He had been down on the Mackenzie for six years, and in the interval a fire let loose by some idiot had swept the Irvine Creek flat and burned Faille's old cabin. "I had some idea of coming back here," he said, "but not now, not after this. It was a perfect country—all a man could wish for—and now look at it! It was so beautiful here, before."

The next morning all of Faille's stuff and all of ours was in his cache, and he disappeared northwards, with his pack on his back, up the long trough of Irvine Creek that runs through to the Upper Nahanni. Good luck to him wherever his trails may lead! We crossed the river, cached the canoe and started westward, through the burned muskeg toward the first of the granite ranges.

A couple of days later I left camp late in the evening and followed the stream up a stony coulee that came down from the mountain to the south of camp. The coulee lay deep in the evening shadow. I turned and climbed up to the western rim, up a fresh slide of broken granite, over small grassy ledges where the gentians grew. The sudden blaze of the sunset light was dazzling for a moment; I sat down on a slab of granite and took out the old Zeiss monocular that has seen so much in its time.

Below and to the west lay a gently undulating plateau of granite, cut by streams into small valleys with low, easy divides. Beyond it lay a range of weirdly shaped mountains; fantastic and unreal they seemed, outlined against the setting sun. There was a slight weather haze that split the evening rays into a thousand particles, and in that golden glory of light I saw a strange thing—a great bay in the mountains and in that bay, an isolated tower of rock so shaped that it looked like a black column of smoke, evil and menacing. Behind those mountains, and set back perhaps another 10 or 15 miles, a second range of serrated peaks showed faintly—the Yukon boundary that must be, for the map was of little use to us here. "Mountainous country—unmapped," was all it had to say, and the Flat River ran through it as a dotted line. To the southwest the plateau sloped up to a skyline, perhaps three miles away, and crossing that skyline the glass showed me two caribou alternately grazing and breaking into short, fast runs.

They seemed to be worried about something. Wolves? Away down below lay the sleeping camp, set by its blue alpine lake among the last dwarf firs of timberline. Mountains lay to the east and to the north—but the light was fading now, and it was time to be getting down to the shelter of that little clump of firs. The great moment had gone and the glory was departed, leaving a memory that could never fade.

A few days later Curtis and I set out westward over the plateau. We planned to go as far west as we could, getting back to camp by nightfall. It was a fine country to travel over. Great stretches of it were open moorland. There were small valleys and meadows of good grazing for the string of pack horses we wished we had. Here and there were groups of small firs or willow, and over much of the country the dwarf "black birch" grew thinly; where it was thick we had another and more vivid name for it.

The streams flowed crystal clear, over sparkling granite gravel—
and through all this ran the caribou trails, wide, easy to follow
and beautifully engineered.

We lunched by a stream at the head of a sheltered pocket in
the hills, and there we left the tea-pail and the outfit, all ready
for supper, and pushed on. At a small lake, set amongst gentian,
ragwort and grass of Parnassus, I stopped to change a film. Curtis
passed on over a ridge and out of sight, and when I followed
over that ridge there was only the great grey-green upland and
no Curtis. Time went by—it was late afternoon now—and I
perched on a huge outcropping of granite and waited: to shout

would have been a waste of time in that big, empty country. A sparrow twittering on a pebble . . .

Finally he reappeared, steaming up out of the valley that lay between us and the western range, and we made our last move forward—we knew now that we had reached the turning point. Across the new valley, and not too far away, lay the great coulee and the black tower. The coulee was cut across by a geological fault and, now that it was unattainable, Curtis knew for a certainty that it held the lost Nahanni gold. Gold? That was nothing! Rubies, roc's eggs and the onyx stone—anything the heart might desire. Sadly we turned our backs on all these riches and headed back on the long trail to supper and on to camp.

A couple of days were spent at the Irvine Creek camp before we headed down the Flat. On one of those I went to the top of a cone-shaped mountain that lay to the northeast to get a panorama of pictures. A thunderstorm blacked the country out for me so I dropped down a thousand feet to the nearest trees, cut myself a shelter beneath an old fir, and made tea and ate some bannock and cheese. Facing page: Albert Faille, 1951. When the rain stopped I climbed up to the ridge again, but thunderstorms were still stalking over the surrounding country and it was not till 8:00 P.M. that I could get the pictures I wanted. I passed the time of waiting in watching, with the glass, a grizzly away up on the far slope of the little valley of the fir trees. He was digging out a marmot; the clods and rocks flew right and left, and presumably he got his marmot in the end, for he ambled off, most contentedly, up the mountainside, over a ridge and out of sight. It was a longish way back to camp, so in the end I got benighted for my pains, and put in a few hours of nightmarish slumber under a thick spreading spruce on the flats of Irvine Creek, huddled in an old shooting jacket with a small fire at my feet.

Meanwhile, the others had taken the canoe up the Flat River, fishing and geologizing. At Faille's old cabin site they came on a wonderful stand of raspberries and were well stuck into this when Curtis heard a noise like a sneeze and Frank distinctly heard the hiss of a snake. They turned and looked toward each other and were surprised to see, right in line between them, a grizzly standing on his hind legs, equally surprised and looking from one to the other. The grizzly was the first to crack. He gave one more sneeze and then dropped on all fours and beat it out of the raspberry thicket. As he ran he bashed into a tall, slender, fire-killed spruce with his shoulder. The dry top whipped forward and snapped, and came down on his rump, and with a startled roar the bear bounded forward and disappeared. Taking it all round, things may be said to have gone off very smoothly on this occasion. The grizzly must have been asleep in the berry patch when Curtis and Frank got there, and it was just a piece of luck that neither of them walked right onto him.

Down the jade-green water of the Flat River, down many a riffle, slid the canoe and we came, in a couple of days, to the mouth of the Flat and to Faille's original cabin of 1927, where I had been the solitary guest at the house-warming supper in that far-off September. Where the Flat enters the Nahanni, the former river is dead slow and the latter very fast. A quarter of a mile down the Nahanni, and on the same side as the Flat, the Raven's Riffle, with its big, white-capped waves, lies in wait for the unwary. One must paddle out of the slack water and into the Nahanni current at top speed, and cross the Nahanni above the riffle, thus gaining the inside of the bend and the easier water. We came out of the Flat River a little short on speed and for a brief space we enjoyed the exhilarating spectacle of the big waves of the Raven's Riffle from far too close as we lurched downstream to meet them, broadside on. But we straightened out just in time, slid through the edge of the rough water, and left the riffle booming under its cliff while we swept on downriver in the wake of a swimming caribou.

For three days we camped at the Gate, that strange place of deep shadows and silent, eddying water. You can lie there on the moss and the blueberry buses, on the rim of the pillar of the Gate, and stretch out an arm and drop a stone sheer, almost a thousand feet, into the river.

An easy day's run brought us down through the Second Canyon and into Deadmen's Valley, and there we camped on the site of the cabin that Gordon Matthews and I had built for the winter of 1928–29. The same tall spruce looked down on the clearing—taller now, so that the midday sun barely reached that spot at all—but cabin and cache were gone. They had vanished so completely that it was hard even for me to say where they had been. The young spruce, the wild roses and the cranberries had taken over, and the creek, in some bygone flood, had swept away the doghouse. Not one thing remained to mark the site except the stout top of our four-ring, collapsible cookstove that lay there in the deep moss—a mute and rusty souvenir of many a good feed.

But, if the buildings had vanished, our hunting trails, we found, were still plain and easy to travel—kept open by the game. We followed the mountain trail to timberline under the spurs of the Tlogo-Tsho Range, and we followed the river trail up into the snyes where some old, old cabins are hidden away, the work of Klondikers, perhaps.

They are built of upright logs, and have fireplaces of clay and stone set in the centre of their floors. They stand amongst tall, black spruce from which hang long, venerable beards of grey-green moss. A sense of eld and of decay and of tragedy pervades that haunted spot. Nothing would induce me to camp there, and I have often wondered what fate overtook the builders of those cabins and left behind that chill feeling of horror that comes over one there, even in the glittering sunlight of a winter's day.

We travelled up the Dry Canyon, into a barren, shut-in world of water-worn stone where no bird sang and no stream flowed to break the silence. We climbed the Little Butte at the outlet of Deadmen's Valley. From its crest we could size up the Cache Rapid that we had to run to pass from the valley into the Lower Canyon, and we could turn and look back upstream to Second Canyon Mountain and the line of spruce on the north bank of the Nahanni where the McLeods had been killed.

Facing page: Patterson and Matthews's cabin in 1928, at -44° F.

The Cache Rapid, or George's Riffle, found us at the parting of the ways. Curtis and Frank had decided to run it, with the big canoe, on the left. I was always a stickler for old established custom and, since I had been told that my old trail down the right bank of the riffle was now impossible owing to a recent rockfall from the canyon wall, I had decided to prove that it

could still be done. Both parties planned to land, they on the island and I in the eddy behind the rockfall, and walk ahead and look the situation over.

We passed Ram Creek and the Little Butte and shot past Starke's Rock and down the upper riffles in famous style. I was in the lead with our 16-foot canoe, and I swung into the eddy behind the rockslide, turned upstream and looked around for the others. There they went, past the island and going at racehorse speed! Curtis was shouting something, but the uproar of the Nahanni made hearing difficult. It sounded like "to hell with looking!" I saw the big canoe rise on a wave, and Frank, paddling bow, made a complete air stroke. They vanished down the hill of water into a turmoil of white—an exhilarating sight and I wouldn't have missed it for anything.

All right—to hell with looking!—and I headed the little canoe downstream, close to shore. The pace quickened and all went well till a rock about the size of an average trapping cabin loomed up with the whole force of the Nahanni pouring over it. The channel between it and the shore was full of sharp rocks, so I swung out about 45 degrees and missed the rock but caught the wash from it on the side. This had the effect of turning the canoe broadside on to the Nahanni—a novel experience for me, and one that I can do without in future. This state of affairs lasted for three waves and three desperate heaves of the paddle. I had things straightened out in time for the big waves at the foot of the riffle and climbed into view of the others over a wave so big that, according to Curtis, I was hidden and only the bottom of the canoe was visible. "We were just coming up," he called out, "to pick up any stray limbs and any useful junk that might come floating down to us!"

Our next camp was halfway through the Lower Canyon, at the mouth of Patterson Creek, and from there we took a day and climbed up the creek gulch to the plateau that lies 4,000 feet above the Nahanni. The Chinook wind was singing over those high prairies, quartz crystals glittered in the gravel beds, autumn had turned "the green, flower-starred upland" of my July 1928 diary to its September browns and reds. And once again one was sad when "evening drove me down into the valley of the great stones, and from there into the trees of the sub-Arctic forest, and so back to camp on the Nahanni." That was written in 1928. Listen a moment to 1951: "Hit out after breakfast up Patterson Cr. Strong S. W. wind. Took photos of creek gulch and the high plateau country. Saw two wolves. Home about 8.00 P.M." How one changes! The very same trip

Facing page: The Lower Canyon.

required two and a half closely written foolscap pages in 1928!

The Nahanni, too, is no longer young. That stretch of the plateau was covered with sheep droppings in 1928; in 1951 there was not a sign of any kind except a very occasional old track. The wild game, from observation and from all reports, has been cut, in 25 years, to one third of its former plenty—probably even less. Various cycles of scarcity have probably coincided with an increased wolf population, better rifles in general use and a greater pressure from mankind. And the paw of the ape has been laid heavily on that lovely river. Much of the Splits country has been devastated by fire in recent years, and all of the Second Canyon—eight miles of the most magnificent river scenery—wrecked, a desert of scarred and fire-blasted rock and scree. A shadowy place of moss-grown precipice and timbered flat it used to be, with stunted spruce and birch rooted in the clefts, growing from every ledge, adorning the islands. But we shall not see that again. Fireweed and ragwort and goldenrod, the wild rose and the willow, are all at work building up humus for future trees. But not in our time.

Homo sapiens, it seemed, had been trying to ascend the Nahanni that very summer, and his traces greeted us when we landed to make camp at the Twisted Mountain. Before this was possible, Frank and I had to burn or heave into the river a collection of cartons, newspapers and tin cans that would have done credit to any National Park campground in the tourist season. Civilization was evidently coming closer.

Facing page: Devastation as the result of a forest fire.

And here we were, down on the Liard again, on the long

trail south—and the Nahanni summer was over. The rush of the river under the nose of Cooper's scow was certainly very soothing . . .

To the north the Mackenzie Mountains still marched by, shining in the moonlight. The Mountains of Youth they would always be for me, and when, I wondered sleepily, would I be seeing them again? Soon, I decided, and the sooner the better—there was not time for another 23 years to go by.

That moon was behaving in an extremely undignified manner. The stars, too—dancing—there could be no doubt about that—but one would have expected better things of the moon . . .

Inadvertently I closed one eye—and then the other . . . 🔲

Fur-traders and Gold Miners

We Clomb the Pathless Pass

The Beaver, Winter 1960

Some 12 miles south of the town of Jasper, Alberta, and close to the main Lake Louise highway, the Whirlpool River flows into the Athabasca. Cars and their human freight rush past this confluence unheeding, but the rare motorist who pauses and walks down to the water's edge may well reflect that he stands on historic ground. For it was at this spot that the old trail of the fur-traders crossed the Athabasca River and took off up the Whirlpool for the Athabasca Pass—and beyond to the Wood River and Boat Encampment on the Columbia. A trail that is now rarely used, in places fallen-in and hard to find, but once a highway plainly marked by the feet of hundreds of men and horses. Fur-trader and priest, botanist, artist, and surveyor, they all went that way in the early days, and they travelled that rough road because they had to: there was no other practicable way to navigable water on the Columbia, and the Peigans had closed the Howse Pass to the south.

The east end of the portage, the meeting of the waters, is, according to Alexander Ross, who crossed the pass with George Simpson in 1825: "at a place called the Hole, from the depth of the water at the edge of the bank, the Athabasca being unfathomable there. Punch Bowl Creek [the Whirlpool River of today], swelled at last to the size of a moderate river . . . discharges itself into the Athabasca at the Hole." Since

Facing page: Pack horse crossing a creek.

the North Westers were first on the scene, most of the names were originally French: the Hole was le Trou and the Whirlpool was la Rivière du Trou. From the Hole to the west end of the portage—to Portage Point on the bank of the Columbia, later to be known as Boat Encampment—is 45 miles as the crow flies; on that, too, our motorist can reflect as he climbs back into his car and drives away south, since for him, by road to Boat Encampment, it will be close on 300.

But miles as the crow flies are not to be met with in the mountains. Alexander Ross estimated the distance at 85 miles. George Simpson made it a bit less: on October 19th, 1824, he noted that they arrived at Boat Encampment "having disposed of the celebrated Athabasca Portage, which altho not exceeding from Jaspers House 120 miles and from Henry's House 80 to 90 occupied us six Days in crossing." That would make the distance from the Hole 75 miles and, having myself carried a heavy pack down the Whirlpool in summer—crossing and recrossing the river on foot, balancing on logs and tussocks in the swampy places, turning and twisting in the bush and around the deadfall—I am inclined to agree with that estimate.

Simpson made that October trip with horses, but even so, things were not easy. Eight inches of snow fell on his party in the night at l'Encampement du Fusil, a meadow on the upstream side of the stony wash of Kane Creek. Above the *battures*, or gravel flats, of the Whirlpool much of the trail is bad going, and Simpson writes: "toward the height of land the Road is as bad and dangerous as it can well be and Glaciers are seen which have bidden defiance to the rays of the Sun since the beginning of time." To the voyageurs there was nothing friendly about these mountain fastnesses. Rather was there something hostile and appalling in the snowy peaks and alpine solitudes—and Ross Cox, camped in early June of 1817 on the height of land, writes: "One of our rough-spun, unsophisticated Canadians, after gazing upwards for some time in silent wonder, exclaimed with much vehemence, 'I'll take my oath, my dear friends, that God Almighty never made such a place!'"

In the whole history of the Canadian fur trade there can be few trails that have occasioned so much physical effort and endurance as has that of the Athabasca Portage. Back east the voyageurs could remember Grand Portage and could boast of their feats of carrying on Portage la Loche. But there were well-beaten trails over those, steep though they were, and no drowning rivers to ford and ford again, no alpine pass at timberline. And in the west there were other passes over the Great Divide—one of them only 40 miles away to the northwest, the route by the Miette River and Buffalo Dung Lake, later to be known as Yellowhead Lake. But this pass, though 2,000 feet lower than the Athabasca Pass, led only to the rough headwaters of the Fraser and the New Caledonia posts.

About the Athabasca Portage, however, there was something dramatic, some epic quality that inspired many of the men who travelled it to write the saga of its trail. It lay, too, on the very lifeline of the fur trade. Eastward in April or May came the express from Fort Vancouver, men wading in icy water, toiling upwards in deep, wet snow. Westward in October came the express from York Factory and the newcomers to the Columbia— their horses slipping and stumbling in the narrow defiles below Kane Creek, snatching at the grass in the lovely meadows north of the Committee's Punch Bowl, sliding dangerously down the Grande Côte to the gravel bars of the Wood River.

Edward Ermatinger came that way from the east in early October of 1827 with a 54-horse outfit. He knew the trail well, having crossed over that very spring with the express from Fort Vancouver to York Factory, and he had perfect weather. With these advantages, it took him only four days from the Hole to Portage Point, and that included picking up various odds and ends on the way—one of his hunters a grizzly by the Punch Bowl, and another a marten on the Grande Côte. Coming through the points of woods and the swampy three miles toward the Columbia River, his 54 horses, he says, churned the trail into "one mire from beginning to end."

The hardest traverse was from west to east, since that was made almost always on foot and included the ascent of the Grande Côte—the Big Hill where the trail climbed steeply for 3,000 feet from the battures of the Wood River into the alpine country. And the worst season was the spring, the months of April and May when the snow still lay deep and soggy in the bush on the Wood River, and the high meadows by the Punch Bowl were still under eight or ten feet of wind-packed snow. On this the travellers had to make their camps, and into it their fires sank while they slept, forming fire-pits with vertical walls of yellow, smoke-stained ice.

Leaving Fort Vancouver about the first of April, the fur-traders would ascend the Columbia River by canoe to the very tip of the Big Bend and there, on Portage Point, which is between the mouths of the Wood and Canoe rivers and some two miles from the modern highway, they would lay up their canoes, cache all they did not need or could not carry and arrange their loads—90 pounds for the Company plus a man's blanket and gun and whatever else he carried for himself. When all was done and an inventory made of the cached stuff, they started up the Wood River, which then was the Portage River.

They started with three miles of swampy ground, and then they hit the First Point of Woods—a place where there is no passage on the opposite bank and where the timber on the trail side comes right to the water's edge. Through this bush they had to struggle with their loads—those who had them using their *pas d'ours*, their bear-paw snowshoes. Edward Ermatinger writes that "the road being hard to find wastes time" and suggests that the horse party in the fall blaze the trees plainly from their saddles high up above snow level. As that was in April of 1827, the year he returned in October with the 54 horses, no doubt he had it done.

Then they came to a six-mile stretch of open gravel flats through which the Portage River flows swiftly in many channels, winding from wall to wall of the valley. Here they had to ford continuously, and they travelled in the icy water almost as much as they did on the bars. Alexander Ross marked these traverses of the Portage on his staff: by nightfall on the first day he had notched up 62 crossings—and there were a few earlier ones not recorded!

On this same stretch of flats, the Governor, George Simpson, records fording the main stream 41 times. In order to breast the strong current they formed a chain with a tall and strong man in the lead, then a small man, and then a big one again and so on. Their heavy loads helped to anchor them against the rushing water, and if a small man was swept off his feet the giants on either side were there to hold him. This living chain would enter the water diagonally to the course of the river so that the full force of the current would not strike vertically on the chain and so break it in the middle. The water was the spring run-off—melting snow and ice—and sometimes their clothes froze on them between fordings, but they had no choice of ways and so drove themselves on, knowing that beyond the mountains, horses and canoes awaited them.

It was on these battures that some of the Iroquois got drunk, and one threw his load of provisions into the river. The Governor's reactions were not slow: soaked, half-frozen and enraged, he took a hatchet and smashed a keg of rum into the river also—just to show "the people" precisely on which side their bread was buttered. We hear no more of trouble.

The next day on that trip of Simpson's was April 24th, 1825. They got through the Second Point of Woods and to the second stretch of battures, where they forded the river 17 times before 6:00 A.M. Then they tackled the Grande Côte and got to the top of the hill at 5:00 P.M. after 12 hours walking, "every Man in the Camp lame and exhausted."

It was Gabriel Franchère, the Astorian, who found the vivid phrase for the arduous travel in the park-like country above the Big Hill. At 6,000 feet the snow lay deep and soft in May 1814, and Franchère writes: "We were obliged to follow exactly the traces of those who had preceded us, and to plunge our legs up to the knees in the holes they had made, so that it was as if we had put on and taken off, at every step, a very large pair of boots."

Franchère was impressed by the great rock that towers above the pass on the northeast: it was "like a fortress of rock," he says, "and had the summit covered with ice." That was McGillivray's Rock—named, Ross Cox notes, in honour of William McGillivray, a principal director of the North West Company. That is by no means certain: a strong case can be made out that it was named for William's younger brother, Duncan, who may have crossed the Athabasca Pass some ten years ahead of David Thompson, the official discoverer in 1811.

Another commentator on the tremendous depth of snow was John McLeod who travelled east through the Athabasca Pass with the express in late April of 1826. His young son, Malcolm, was also of the party. They left Boat Encampment on April 27th and John McLeod notes in his diary: "Snow so deep, obliged to cut our leather trousers into snow shoes." Malcolm records that the snow was 15 feet deep at the foot of the pass and 30 at the summit. His father wrote: "We clomb the pathless Pass: resting at night literally, at times, on the tops of the trees." To the east of the Divide the "snow diminished fast in depth till at Jasper House it was nearly gone . . . arrived 5 May, just a week in the struggle . . . even the boy suffered not."

Returning now to Simpson's 1825 party, they left their high camp at 3:30 A.M., roused by the thunder of avalanches, and they came at 6:00 to the Committee's Punch Bowl, the little lake that sits right on the Divide and sends its waters in opposite directions to two far distant oceans. That was the summit of the Athabasca Pass, 5,724 feet above the level of the sea, and there, according to custom, "the people had a Glass of Rum each and ourselves a little Wine and Water which was drunk to the Health of their Honors with three Cheers. At 9 got to the Camp Fusil where we put up to breakfast and rested till 12 A.M." And at 6:00 P.M. they made camp on the Grande Batture, "every Man of the party knocked up." They must have been men of iron to get that far under those conditions and with those loads.

The Grande Batture of the Whirlpool River is good walking, open and level, covered with a soft mat of the dryas flower. But, though the snow was less deep, they were not yet down to bare ground, and Simpson writes under April 26th: "Never did exhausted travellers turn out less disposed to renew a toilsome Journey then we did at 3 o'clock this Morn, every man . . . requiring the aid of a Walking Stick our feet being much blistered and Lacerated by the rough Travel on the Battures and in the Bed of the River; we however improved as we got Warm upon it . . ." But their troubles were coming to an end, for at 10:00 A.M., having already forded the Rivère du Trou 27 times, they came to l'Encampement d'Orignal (the Halfway Camp of today near the forks of the Middle Whirlpool), and there they found two men waiting for them with the horses. Gratefully they breakfasted, mounted and rode on toward the still-distant Hole.

They rode far—and the following day found them away down the Athabasca at what Alexander Ross calls Rocky Mountain House—which was Jasper's House. There, an old North Wester was in charge, Joseph Felix Larocque, and there they took to canoes. "Wherever there is a northwester in this country," Ross writes, "the birch-rind canoe is sure to be found. Although boats would have been far more safe and suitable for our purpose, yet we had to embark in those fragile shells to shoot a dangerous stream."

No matter: safe or unsafe, they were on their way—afloat once more on the element that was home to them, and in the frail craft that had given them the mastery of it. The Athabasca Portage lay behind them. 🔲

Trail to the Big Bend

The Beaver, Spring 1960

Nobody seems to know just who started it. But to the prospector far pastures always look green, and since at least as early as 1861 men had been working slowly northward up the Columbia River, panning as they went, finding enough gold to lure them on. Then rumours began to come from out of that dim forest country—rumours of shallow diggings on the Big Bend. The Northwest was suddenly galvanized into activity: Portland and Victoria each had visions of a golden future in which, for each, the rival city had no share: from Cariboo to California the optimists and the restless ones hit the trail—and by the first months of 1865 the short-lived rush was on.

Forewarned by the increasing activity of the previous four years, the Hudson's Bay Company had already taken steps to secure a share in the new trade; and on November 14th, 1864, Chief Factor Roderick Finlayson was able to write from Victoria to Chief Trader Joseph Wm. McKay at Kamloops: "We note that Mr. Martin is stationed for the winter at the East end of Lake Souswap and that you had pre-empted a section of land there for the Company." Mr. Martin's tenure of office was not a long one: by the summer of 1865 his accounts were in disorder and he was replaced at this post by Mr. Sabiston. The post in question was at the head of the long northern arm of Shuswap Lake, now called Seymour Arm.

Facing page: Shuswap Lake, BC.

In April 1865, William Downie led a party from Colville in Washington Territory to the Big Bend country. This party included H.C. Carnes, and Downie and Carnes creeks, powerful streams flowing down from the Selkirks, remain as memorials to these men. At Carnes Creek they discovered gold in paying quantities—"gold in the shape of cucumber seed, coarse and dark-coloured." They pushed on upriver, investigating Goldstream, French and McCulloch creeks. They found that French Creek gold was "rough, flat and very bright." Late in October they returned south to Washington Territory.

This was only one of many such parties, and from them the most optimistic reports trickled down to Victoria and Portland. The *British Colonist* newspaper of Victoria recorded them all. On September 21st, 1865, under the headline "Encouraging News," we read that ". . . diggings paying $16 to $18 a day have been struck." And on October 5th that "A Mr. Baxter of Yale left French Creek on the 19th ult., travelling time from the Columbia River to Yale, six days! Great confidence prevailed, he said. Claims were down to bedrock and there were expectations of from 30 to 40 oz. a day to the hand . . . Mr. McCulloch had discovered McCulloch's Creek and expected it to be as rich as French Creek." In the issue of November 30th there were again "Cheering Reports. The Half-breed Co. (French Creek) is taking out as high as 6 oz. to the pan a few feet from the surface—now 25 to 65 oz. a day." One man, Dupuis, took out $5,000 on French Creek and then quit. Five hundred dollars of this was in a single day. Nuggets were being found on French Creek "of from $15 to $20 apiece." Best of all was a report in The *British Columbian*, reprinted in the *Colonist* of December 14th, from a

Mr. Richard Edwards ". . . alias Brother Dick, and just arrived from McCulloch's Creek. We may premise that Mr. Edwards is an honest, cautious miner who will not knowingly exaggerate, and whose every word will be implicitly believed by those who know him. His Clemens Company took out 12 to 35 oz. per day before they quit and on the last day our informant took out $105 in one pan." The largest nugget found by the Clemens Company weighed one and a half ounces. French Creek dust, The *Portland Oregonian* tells us: ". . . assays $18.50 to the ounce and commands $17 from the traders."

Somehow or other all this activity had to be supplied with food and other essentials, and the diggings had to be made accessible to incoming miners. Two routes led into the Big Bend country: one from Washington Territory by way of the Columbia River and the Arrow Lakes; and the other by way of Kamloops Lake, the Thompson River and Shuswap Lake, and thence by trail over the Gold Range to the Columbia. The government surveyors, Walter Moberly with Turnbull and Green, were busy throughout 1865, locating the trail over the Gold Range, surveying a townsite at the head of Seymour Arm and around the little Hudson's Bay Company post there, and exploring the Eagle Pass through which the CPR now runs— then, as now, the easiest trail from the Shuswap country to the Columbia but too far south to be of much use in this gold rush. Moberly, incidentally, disallowed the HBC pre-emption at the head of the lake, reserving the whole of it for government purposes. The site when surveyed was variously named: it was called Ogden City, and sometimes "Ogdensville . . . so named after the Hudson's Bay Company's factor there" (*Colonist*,

October 5th, 1865). No trace of this name in connection with this post can be found in the Company's records, and the name that came into general use was that of Seymour, or Seymour City, after Frederick Seymour, then Governor of the Crown Colony of British Columbia.

The surveyors—as is usual with surveyors—had their troubles. Turnbull and Herman, working on the Columbia, became impatient with their Indians who refused to work on Sundays. "Last Sunday they attempted to work a bark canoe by themselves, ran their feet through the bottom of the canoe—saved all except some blankets. They are now awaiting the arrival of the Indians, into whose hands they will again have to consign themselves."

The boat builders were busy, too. Throughout the summer of 1865, in an effort to secure the traffic for the American route, Captain White was building his boat, the *Forty-Nine*, at Colville, Washington Territory. It was hoped that she would make her trial trip in September—and then in October. Finally, in late November a correspondent of the *Colonist* wrote that she was at last completed. "She was built," he adds, "two miles from the H.B.Co.'s old fort and sixteen miles from the American fort at Colville. All is excitement here, men are leaving every day in small boats for the mines." In the following day's *Colonist* a miner from Cariboo, headed for Blackfoot (in what is now Idaho), describes Colville as "one of the meanest places a man ever got out of, being inhabited chiefly by thieves." According to him the new steamer was nearly finished "and the Colville folks think she will knock the Thompson River route into a cocked hat next spring"—an opinion that was wholeheartedly shared by

The *Portland Oregonian*, which saw fit to add "There is but one objection that can now be urged against Boat Encampment—it is in British Territory."

Meanwhile the Hudson's Bay Company had not been idle. In June 1865, Chief Trader W.A. Mouatt was ordered to Fort Kamloops to "examine Thompson's River and Suschwap Lakes, ascertaining the facilities on those waters for navigating a Steamboat." His report on the river was favourable and he also observed that the Company's post at the head of "Suschwap Lake . . . is in a very advantageous position, owing to its proximity to the trail leading over the 'Divide' and also to its being in the neighbourhood of the only large quantity of timber on the Lake." That is interesting in view of the many good stands of timber existing on the lake today.

Roderick Finlayson, knowing the habits of rivers, wrote again on October 11th to McKay at Kamloops: ". . . before you return to Yale [you are to] examine carefully, the depth of water and the breadth of the channel in the shallowest parts of the river between the Kamloops and Souswap Lakes and report the same to us . . . this examination to be made when the water is at its lowest stage in the River." McKay was also ordered to secure to the Company the lands pre-empted both at "Savonah ferry" (which was near the outlet of Kamloops Lake) and also at the head of "Souswap Lake." In view of the probably heavy traffic in the spring of 1866, provisions of all kinds were to be accumulated at Kamloops, particularly "potatoes grain and dried fish."

Reports on the low-water stage of the Thompson must have been favourable, since the Company went ahead with its plans and had the SS *Marten* built that winter at Savona's Ferry by a Mr. Wright. In addition, a whole fleet of small boats was constructed on the shores of both the big lakes by private individuals and syndicates.

The trail over the Gold Range from Seymour to the Columbia near Downie Creek was well trodden by this time. It was known as Moberly's Trail; there was good horse feed on the Shuswap slope of the range though nothing much on the Columbia side. In July 1865 the Indians drove 30 to 40 head of pack horses across. Smith and Ladner organized a regular pack-train service from Seymour to the Columbia. They hired all the Indians they could lay hands on to pack stuff in: 20 Indians started on October 11th with packs of 60 to 100 pounds. Ten head of Smith and Ladner beef cattle were met that fall crossing the summit. Today, the queerest landmark of all on that long-forgotten trail is a dump of slabs for two pool tables that were somehow struggled in over the pass. What happened? Did some miner, returning broke, bring the news that the bubble had burst just as the packers reached the summit with their awkward loads?

From time to time came editorials in The *British Colonist* shouting for all the trade "via Yale, Kamloops and Mr. Wright's new steamer," pointing out that the total distance from Victoria was one third less than that from Portland and listing the amenities of travel—the HBC steamer *Labouchere* from San Francisco to Victoria—fast river steamers to Yale—and then "to Savana Ferry, 133 miles, a splendid Government Wagon Road and Comfortable way-side Houses every few miles; over the road travellers can easily walk, or they can ride in Barnard's Fast

Four-Horse Stages. From Savana Ferry the Hudson's Bay Co.'s new and swift steamer *Marten* will run to Ogden City . . . a distance of 111 miles. From Ogden City to the Columbia River, a distance of 34 miles, there is an excellent Government Pack Trail."

Everybody did his best to climb on the bandwagon. In the *Colonist* for February 15th, 1866, there is a rather pathetic little advertisement: "No one," it says, "should start for these mines without being quite sure that his teeth are in order. F. W. Cave, Dentist, Trounce Alley . . . is still practising his profession at English prices."

In April 1866, activity became feverish. The lakes were now free of ice. A thousand miners were reported on their way up the Columbia from Colville. Freight from Savona's Ferry to Seymour was three cents a pound. "Mr. Steinberger of Yale will start a brewery at Big Bend—the utensils required having already gone forward." Reports came through of new creeks running $7 to $9 to the pan. "Cottonwood Smith has discovered a direct trail from Seymour to French Creek, so cutting off 30 miles from the government trail." (One more "discovery" of this magnitude and the Columbia River would have been flowing directly into Shuswap Lake!)

The *Marten* was launched on May 10th, 1866, and spent the next two weeks at Savona's Ferry, installing machinery. She left on her first trip to Seymour on May 26th, and her arrival is vividly described in a letter to the *Colonist* (June 4th) from "W.E.O."

"Seymour City. May 27. 1866 . . . steamer *Marten* coming round the point and delighting the eyesight of every Seymourite as she . . . glided through the noble waters of Shuswap Lake.

Five hundred hungry pioneers about that time were partaking of their evening dose of beans and bacon, but at the sight of the steamer they hurriedly cast pots and pannikins aside and soon the roar of mighty cannonading was heard emanating from the efforts of the Royal Anvil Artillery . . . Every available explosive weapon was brought to bear so that the steamer might receive a hearty welcome. Three rousing cheers and a tiger rent the air . . ." The passengers responded in kind. Speeches of welcome were made by the Seymourites—but their efforts were as nothing to the response of the commander of the *Marten* who caused champagne and HBC rum to flow freely for the benefit of all hands on board and of "every individual who stood on the beach." Marvellous days! We shall not see their like again.

A wonderful trip through the beautiful Thompson River country had been enjoyed by all, including the Indians "who were almost frantic at the sight of a steamer and rode furiously along the banks trying to keep up with her."

That was the high point. The stage was now set for a magnificent gold rush; the only fly in the ointment was that the boom had already bust. Already in May, in spite of boosting editorials in the *Colonist*, doubts were arising. Bedrock was deep and on McCulloch Creek it was pitching; the spring was late in that deep snow country. By June the creeks were steadily rising and there were reports of flooding. A letter from French Creek advised miners not to come without four or five hundred dollars "as jawbone [or credit] is pretty well played out."

The *Forty-Nine* was now making her trips to La Porte, which was one mile above the mouth of Downie Creek and on the west bank of the Columbia. From there freight was lined up through the rapids to Wilson's Landing and then packed by men or horses to the navigable part of Goldstream River. Thence it was taken by canoes and small boats upstream to the mouths of the gold-bearing creeks and once again backpacked by men—in the case of French Creek two miles up to the store. It just simply could not be done; prices were too high and men were leaving the country. The huge piles of water-worn boulders on French Creek remain, mute testimony to the struggles of relays of miners for their hard-won gold.

Even W.E.O., that confirmed optimist, admits to difficulties. Under the heading "Prospects of the Country" he writes: "Notwithstanding the many disappointed, sore footed, light pocketed . . . bootless and pantless specimens of the *genus homo* returning from Seymour, every one must feel quite satisfied that despite the drawbacks of a very late and severe season, these mines will turn out to be the great Eldorado of British Columbia."

W.E.O.'s account of the town of 500 and its buildings, which included six saloons, thirteen stores, five bakeries, three restaurants, etc., etc., "to say nothing of a coffee and doughnut stand," is of interest when one has walked over the site. There is nothing there now to mark all this activity, absolutely nothing— just a few holes that once were cellars, the sandy shore and the tall forest trees.

There must have been a Hudson's Bay Company outpost on French Creek, for on September 20th, 1866, Roderick Finlayson wrote to Chief Trader James Bissett at Kamloops: "As Mr. Moffatt's Services are apparently much required . . . at Kamloops, You will please . . . to order him down from French

Creek, and send Mr. Milne there to replace him leaving Sabiston for the present in charge at Seymour, where there is but little business now doing."

And then, a year later, came the end in a letter from Chief Factor W.F. Tolmie to Moffatt at Kamloops, October 21st, 1867: Sabiston was ordered to Savona's Ferry, but "First of all however the goods, doors, windows, and every other moveable of any value must be removed from Seymour to Kamloops . . . and let the door and window openings in the building at Seymour be boarded up, as we may yet have use for the establishment, of which it might be well to give a trusty Indian charge."

The SS *Marten*, after her one spell of glory, proved not to be a paying proposition. Her government subsidy of $400 a month was discontinued, but she lingered on doing the odd jobs of the district. As late as 1876 she was still on the water, taking Lord and Lady Dufferin from Savona to Kamloops.

The last trip of the *Forty-Nine* for 1866 was made on November 15th from Colville. According to The *Portland Oregonian* only French and McCulloch creeks had paid anything worthwhile, and three quarters of the men who came down on that last trip "did so as dead-heads—broke."

Yet some determined spirits stayed on in those deep, snowy valleys of the Selkirks. A letter from French Creek dated January 31st, 1867, states that two men on Discovery had taken out 175 ounces, but does not say in what time. There were still 75 men on French Creek and 12 on McCulloch. "We have had a very jolly Christmas: we can boast of a skating rink, a dance and a French class." There was a "free ball the other night and a very handsome supper . . . The band was something that might vie with that of the Coldstream Guards, consisting of the following instruments viz guitar, violin (a bully one made on the creek out of soup bouillon tins), tambourine and bones both of home manufacture . . . The Ball was kept up with great zest until nine o'clock the next morning. All the ladies in town were present, they number two and a half."

That little half-lady of French Creek might have been eight years old on that festive night—when no doubt she slept through the small hours on a pile of the dancers' mackinaws, safely tucked away in a corner, wrapped warmly in her blankets. If she were still alive, she would now be over a hundred, so long ago did all this happen. ▨

The Strangest Man I Ever Knew

The Beaver, Spring 1956

Governor George Simpson kept a "Character Book" in which he recorded, under code numbers to which he had the key, his opinions of the officers of the Hudson's Bay Company—opinions that had considerable bearing on their chances of promotion or otherwise. One hopes, for the peace of mind of those concerned, that this book was kept under lock and key—for in its pages no holds were barred and the well-known "graciousness" of the Governor was laid aside; the irritability of the moment was given free play and, consequently, many of the judgments recorded proved later to have been hasty and unjust. In the case of Samuel Black, the explorer of the Finlay River, the dice were loaded against him before ever the Governor took up his pen.

Not for nothing did Black receive, sometime in 1821 from his old associates and partners of the North West Company, a ring on which was engraved, "To the most worthy of the worthy North-westers." By his mere presence at Fort Chipewyan in the early months of 1821, Black had kept Simpson, the newcomer to the fur country, perpetually on the *qui vive*, waiting for the attack that never came. Simpson's men would have been aware of this and he himself would always remember, and hold against Black in the years to come, the alarms and perplexities of that first winter

Facing page: The Finlay River.

at Fort Wedderburn. And so it is with this in mind that we find Simpson writing in his Character Book of 1832 regarding Black:

> No. 11. About 52 years of Age. The strangest Man I ever knew. So wary & suspicious that it is scarcely possible to get a direct answer from him on any point, and when he does speak or write on any subject so prolix that it is quite fatiguing to attempt following him. A perfectly honest man and his generosity might be considered indicative of a warmth of heart if he was not known to be a cold blooded fellow who could be guilty of any cruelty and would be a perfect Tyrant if he had power. Can never forget what he may consider a slight or insult, and fancies that every man has a design upon him. Very cool, resolute to desperation, and equal to the cutting of a throat with perfect deliberation; yet his word when he can be brought to the point may be depended on. A Don Quixote in appearance ghastly, raw boned and lanthorn jawed, yet strong vigorous and active.
>
> Has not the talent of conciliating Indians by whom he is disliked, but who are ever in dread of him, and well they may be so, as he is ever on his guard against them and so suspicious that offensive and defensive preparation seem to be the study of his Life having Dirks knives & loaded Pistols concealed about his person and in all directions about his Establishment

even under his Table cloth at Meals and in his Bed. He would be admirably adapted for the Service of the North West coast where the Natives are so treacherous were it not that he cannot agree with his colleagues which renders it necessary to give him a distinct charge. I should be sorry to see a man of such character at our Council board. Tolerably well Educated and most patient and labourous in whatever he sets about, but so tedious that it is impossible to get through business with him.

The very fact that Simpson, who had met and known so many men and so many queer characters, describes Black as "the strangest Man I ever knew" is in itself a sort of left-handed compliment: it indicates a certain strength of character—or if not that, then at least a union of opposites in one complex human being that merits examination. Black's character shows in his writings, and anyone living with him, on and off for four years or so, as I did while working on his Journal, gradually builds for himself a picture of the man—tall, big-boned and angular, deep-voiced and slow-speaking. To this figure certain mental characteristics attach themselves, one by one: they emerge from the pages of the Journal and they appear between the close lines of minute handwriting in the field notebooks, written in pencil, or in ink that has faded a little, or sometimes in ink that is still as black as it was in 1824 and 1825—notes that were made on the spot, in rain or shine and often *en canoe*. And now and then a glimpse comes to us through the eyes of one who knew him—Simpson, it may be, or McLoughlin;

Black's friend, John Stuart, or his victim, Peter Fidler. And his fellow North Wester and life-long friend, Peter Skene Ogden.

The first thing that emerges from Simpson's Character Book estimate of Black is his tediousness and prolixity. I have wondered whether, in the meetings of these two men after 1821, this was not a form of self-defence on Black's part—a barrier that he erected against a man whom he cannot have liked and who was personally responsible for the temporary exclusion of himself, Ogden and Cuthbert Grant from the fur trade at the union of the two Companies.

Father Morice, the priest-historian-geographer, must have had access to some of Black's private correspondence. From it he draws the conclusion that Black "must have been a good-natured man who saw life through rose-colored glasses and had not a little sense of the ludicrous." Amongst other evidence of this Father Morice cites a letter of Black's to Chief Trader Alexander Fisher. Fisher was in charge of Alexandria and so, in the latter part of his time there, had the misfortune to be sandwiched in between Black and Ogden, next-door neighbour of each and, as the crow flies, 150 miles from either. He was not a likable character: Cuthbert Cumming wrote of him from Chats: ". . . he is a man by no means scruplous in what he says & cares not by what means he obtains the end—it is natural to suppose that a man of his vindictive disposition will blacken the character of every man in this District."

The sort of man, in short, who would automatically arouse the very worst in forthright, outspoken men like Black and Ogden—and Father Morice quotes at length from a letter of Black's, which he regards as a satire on Fisher's "well-known foibles." The letter is dated October 29th, 1832, and starts with some details as to the supply of salmon. Then:

> Lolo [Black's interpreter] tells me of the many tricks wherewith you deceive the Indians, such as making holy water in wash handbasins, dressing up your cook to make him hold it, walking about the house with a whitewash brush in your hand with many mumblings and magical words, sprinkling the natives in said holy water, telling them that if they do not come to your place to dance and bring their furs with them this fall, they will be swallowed up like another Sodom into a fiery furnace or boiling cauldron . . . thereby frightening the Indians from walking on God's earth & going about their usual occupations. However, as some of these poor devils may have resisted such an imposition on their understanding which you practise in order to get their furs, Lolo makes his usual tour among the natives belonging to this district, being instructed by no means or pretence whatever to interfere in any way or trade a single skin from any Indian that has been accustomed to frequent your post. At the same time he is to get information as to the truth of the reports concerning your proceedings, and when he returns and gives me the necessary proofs of so infamous tricks then I will act Accordingly for the general interest of the Honorable Hudson's Bay Company, not to get the Indian's furs for one year, but

always . . . and make truth triumph against
jugglery, tricks and profanations of God's holy
rites and sacraments . . .

A fragment only of Fisher's indignant reply was seen by
Father Morice, ending with the words "I regret to find myself
situated as I am (your neighbor); for it is evident you wish to get
me or yourself into trouble. I have with great caution avoided
you . . ." The Father, who was evidently thoroughly enjoying
this correspondence, regrets the disappearance of the rest of it.
He felt that he was losing something: "were it only the occasion
of a good smile at the expense of the poor, rapacious trader,
who was in dead earnest, whatever may have been Black's real
intentions or meaning."

A thought occurred to me recently—to go again to Black's
field notebooks in the British Columbia Archives and to compare
what he had written there with the final official version of his
Journal—to see, that is, whether he had "written up" the Journal,
adding embellishments from memory, or whether what he had
written for his own eyes alone might not be even more detailed.

As I peered at that small writing, with patience and a
magnifying glass, one definite fact emerged: it was the Journal
that had been cut down, incredible as that may seem to those
who have studied it. Let me give one or two examples:

Journal. May 22nd, 1824 ". . . made a Portage
at a Rapid . . ."

Notebook. Same date. " . . . arrived at a Rapid
made a Portage of 500 Paces over a low flat

point of mica & vains of white clear stone (Quartz) the River runs over a bed of this mica like substance the strata is in scales [word illegible] in leaves or scales small bits like Talk & a few little square bits of yellow harder substance."

This was at the Finlay Rapids at the head of the Peace. The yellow substance in the schist was iron pyrites.

Notebook. May 27th. "The Old Slave and I having debark^d below the Rapid went to the end I think the Canoe can go up w^t some pieces in it untill the last Cape when a Short Portage can be made tho [word illegible] stiff & perpendicular to get up the Cape tho intended by nature for a Portage but the most of the Load must be carried across in which there is some stiff hills & a [inky thumb mark here] set the men (who arrived about 1½ or 2 hours before sunset at the little ense [bay]) about putting their axes in order to cut a Road for no one has ever passed there for I suppose the Iroquois have gone up, without making a Portage perhaps at low water. The Men had a hard pull along the Caps to get to this place they cross^d twice before they got here this place is a surprise to us all as we only heard of its being a Rapid & if the Portage they speak of far from this is as bad in proportion we shall have bad work to get on we are not yet near the place [word illegible] the Portages we will take 5 days more to go but its the Current for we do not now make far in a day sent my Bouts [Bowsman and Sternsman] to examine this place.

[Later, and after trimming his pen] "La Guard & Perreault came back from examining the Rapid & say tho they might go up in the Canoe they think it a risque & want to make the Portage."

This was at Deserters' Canyon, and here the notebook account is *more than twice as long* as the corresponding passage in the Journal, which does not contain the interesting references to the Iroquois, Black's predecessors up the Finlay.

On the following day Black found that Bouché and Ossin had deserted him in the night. Of these men the Journal says, under May 28th: ". . . the former an Old offender and the latter a simpleton & debau[c]hed by the other Scamp Bouche." It is the notebook, however, that adds the human touch: "J.M. Bouche is the Rascal & debauched the other who is also a worthless scamp but a simple devil & thinks to get to his wife at Fort Chipewean." Here also Black records that, in addition to the Company property that Bouche and Ossin stole, they had the effrontery to go off with "Mr. Manson's Pot Crook."

The field notebooks contain accounts of various journeys and end with Black's notes, made for his personal use and with no official report in view, on his trip down the Columbia River in October–November 1825. His terrier-like interest in all visible things is very noticeable here: Indian encampments, geological structures and the gradual appearance

Facing page: Deserters' Canyon.

of the western larch—all are recorded. South of McGillivray's River, which is now the Kootenay, the party travelled "smelling Fish and Eagles all day." One would not smell them now: Grand Coulee Dam in the State of Washington has effectively destroyed the salmon run on the long Canadian section of the Columbia River.

Black was at the Kettle Falls portage on October 28th–29th and devotes three pages to that place, describing the trees, rocks and grassy hills, all of which "appearing in the sweep of View gives Romantic variety to the scene." He is particularly attentive to an old Indian burial ground on a point by the portage:

> . . . at this burial Place or sacrifice Place we find a cluster Head Tombstones set up right

wᵗ small stones keeping them up about these Tombs is painted boards 4 or more feet high red & one white stripe the Tool of the Boards tied in an old mat of rushes and kept up in the Boards by 2 sticks one over each side tied at the ends round these Tombstones & on Poles & Trees near them are hung wᵗ sacrifices their furniture utensils & Bags also a nearly new 2 ½-pt. Blanket a good open Kettle the Pole large driven through its bottom also an Old Callico shirt numbers of small Kettles & an excellent mat made of Goats Wool white wᵗ Colᵈ bass.

It must have been from this collection of kettles dangling like some strange fruit from poles and trees that these falls and the nearby Kettle River got their names.

The next stop was at the Spokane River Forks and here the party got the news that Dr. McLoughlin might be found at "Spokan House." Several of Black's travelling companions promptly took to horse, and Black's diary leaves geology and botany to remark: "Mr. McL[eod] goes himself to meet the Doctor to Intrigue or Jockey me out of my appointment. The Ermatinger Lads have no scruples & will fall in wᵗ his views in rising & propagating something to work on the Doctor but they will fail as the Doctor is too Old a Cock to be taken wᵗ Chaff . . ."

This must be an illustration of Simpson's remark in the Character Book: ". . . fancies that every man has a design upon him." If so, then Black did not take these fancied intrigues very seriously: he evidently had full confidence in the Doctor for he remained with the boats and notes in his diary the return of his companions with their horses all sweated up from a very fast 70-mile ride.

How much Black has to tell us! And, with a little better education, how much more clearly he could have set it down! He was probably a moody man—soured, too, at least for a time, by the fact that he had wasted five of his remaining active years at Nez Perces when he longed, above all things, to be sent on active service "to discover new lands." He may have been all things to all men—a friend of the gay Ogden, a tedious windbag to the Governor, a furious duellist to the naturalist David Douglas, whom he challenged for the honour of the Company. He may have been disliked by the Nez Perces against whom he had to be on his guard, but it was at McLoughlin's orders that he had maintained, and refused to lower, his prices at Fort Nez Perces. Certainly elsewhere and in his writings he shows a strong sympathy for the Indians who, he says, are like children "siting in darkness seeking for light." And it is not a harsh man who would record, on July 14th, 1824, that his Sikanni carriers "made away with all our dried Deers Meat & cast a wistful eye on the Pemican & requires some resolution to resist so many pleased faces."

The end came on February 8th, 1841, at Thompson's River—and on that day this enigmatic man, so wary and suspicious according to Simpson, and so busy with precautions against attack, appears to have taken no notice at all of the Indian who was sitting by the fire in his hall, waiting to kill him. Others were suspicious but not Black, who merely extended to the Indian a little more than the customary hospitality and then went ahead with his own affairs.

This Indian was a nephew of Chief Tranquille who had died shortly before. Tranquille's widow had persuaded the young man that Black's "medicine" had been the cause of her husband's death, and now he was at Thompson's River on a mission of vengeance. Toward evening the Indian was left alone in the hall, when Black passed through on his way to his quarters. The Indian took his gun from its place of concealment in some dark corner and, as Black stooped to pass through a low doorway, he fired and the old fur-trader pitched forward, dead. In the confusion that followed, the Indian escaped from the fort.

Nothing seems to fit in these estimates of Black. They vary too much and often contradict each other. It seems that you either liked the man or disliked him intensely. He aroused no negative feelings.

A sale was held, at Jasper's House in the spring of 1842, of the contents of a trunk of Black's that had got marooned there. Little, unfortunately, is to be learned from the various items. There were shaving implements, a towel, two brushes, soap, two pairs of silk hose (worn), and a braided *surtout*. A clay pipe and a German pipe proclaimed him a smoker, and a "Liquor case, partly furnished" reminds us that he was not a teetotaller. There were odds and ends of clothing, and bits of weapons that may have seen service at Ile-a-la-Crosse—a sword belt, gun implements, one broken double-barrel pistol, a "Garnished Shot pouch," and "I damd. case Matl. Instruments & pistol flask." There were some geological specimens and—of most interest to us today—"vols. pocket Cyclopaedia, 1 dictionary, 1 plated pencil case and 1 portfolio (old)"—the tools of the writer.

There still remains one last question mark—one more facet

to this curious character. This villain, this outlaw and felon—I am quoting George Simpson—took good care of his mother in Scotland. In 1813 and 1814, when he was earning £90 per annum sterling, he sent home to her over £50. Then comes a blank in the records, and then, from 1829–39 inclusive, Black sent his mother various sums, amounting in all to £630. A further order for £100 arrived too late to be paid, for Mrs. Black had died almost a year previously. And £730 of the year 1840, translated into the values of our time, represents a goodly sum.

Nicola, chief of the Okanagans, pronounced Black's funeral oration: ". . . he was kind, just and generous to us," the Indian said, "and I know he loved us."

What exactly did Nicola intend by that? Did he really mean it? Or was it because the ammunition issue had been suspended after Black's murder and it was vital to the Indians that it should be restored?

It is unlikely that we shall ever know. 🔳

Travels, from the West Coast to the Northern Rivers

Province of Infinite Variety

The Beaver, Spring 1958

Passing in one easy day's drive from the forests of the coast to the Interior Plateau of southern British Columbia, you will notice particularly two trees—the cedar and the ponderosa pine. The jungle thins out as you follow the Fraser River upstream, the air becomes lighter and warmer, the cedars become fewer and smaller. Then they disappear except for isolated groups and individual trees hiding high up in some shadowy canyon—and the first pines make their appearance. The road bids farewell to the Fraser at Lytton and turns eastward up the Thompson River. Soon the hillsides are bare and open, and the cliffs and bluffs, tricked out in the flaring colours of the desert, appear to have been scorched by ancient fires. The road twists and climbs upwards on to the benches, and the ghosts of old orchards flit by, skeletons of dead trees, stark and black amidst the olive green of the returning sage. This is the land of the sunflower and the sand rose, the cactus and the rattlesnake: it is the land of bunch-grass and its finest product, the Hereford cow. And, above all, it is the land of the giant pine with its long, shining needles and its great cones. With its snakeskin-pattern bark glowing redly against the young green of the spring meadows or the tawny grass of autumn, this pine is the very emblem of the dry belt. Standing there in the dry warmth beneath the huge branches, it is hard to

Facing page: "... this pine is the very emblem of the dry belt."

believe that only two hundred miles away to the westward lies
Kennedy Lake, long since described by British Columbia's most
famous meteorologist as "the wettest spot in North America."
Yet it is so—and the difference in precipitation is from six inches
per annum at Ashcroft to well over two hundred inches in the
rainforests of Vancouver Island.

Across the province, from west to east, fir and cedar, pine
and spruce fight it out as one crosses range after range of
mountains, passing from rainforest to dry belt to forest again
until, in the end, the trees disappear as the Rockies pile up into
the rooftree of the continent.

The whole vast province is like that—variable, cut to no set
pattern and bewildering to the outlander. It is a matter of choice.
Here in one province a man can travel from the glaciers and the

fiords of the coast, by way of the cattle ranges, the mines and the great lakes of the interior, to the oil and grain lands of the Peace River country—a land that, geographically speaking, has been stolen from Alberta. If you wish to express this change in terms of animals it becomes no less striking, for it involves a transition from the sea otter, the hair seal and the little cream-coloured Kermode bear to the Stone sheep, the moose and the grizzly bear of the Rockies. Even in the skies one can see the change: the soft, vaguely luminous cloudscapes of the Pacific have here given way to the riotously magnificent Chinook skies of the eastern foothills.

Facing page: ". . . the rooftree of the continent."

This page: ". . . the great lakes of the interior."

Passing from north to south the story is the same: it is as if

one were to go, in Europe, direct from Lapland to the southern valleys of Gascony. In the north, in those last strongholds of the wild—the lonely canyons of the Upper Liard—the trapper freights in his supplies with the fall of the leaf. There, through the long winter, he travels over his line plying his indent trade— an anachronism, a survival from a time gone by. In the warm, sun-scorched valleys of the south his fellow British Columbians prune and spray. Upon the trapper in the frozen silence of the north the Dall sheep and the Rocky Mountain goat look down: far above the toiling fruit grower of the southern Okanagan it is the California bighorn who posts his vedettes on the spurs of the Monashee.

My first acquaintance with British Columbia is ancient history now: a job on a dairy farm in the lush, green springtime of the Lower Fraser Valley—a time, on old Sumas Lake, of

hawthorn blossom and of fields of lupins that curled away from the plough in a blue unending wave.

My second view was from outside looking in—from a ranch in Alberta that lay close to the Continental Divide. From that vantage point we were able to reach, with our pack train, parts of the sister province that were not nearly so accessible to the resident British Columbians themselves. That state of affairs lasted for 16 happy years, and as those years went by we came to regard those remote valleys of BC as a natural appanage of Alberta—or, if not quite that, at least as part of BC set aside by a kind providence as a playground for the more active and enterprising of Albertans.

Facing page: ". . . our pack train." This page: ". . . alone with the silence and the sun."

By various passes, in one or two days of mountain travel,

those green fastnesses could be reached. The journey from the high, dry plateau and the windswept foothills of Alberta into the deep, silent valleys of British Columbia—not in a train or a car, but on foot or in the saddle—was, every time, a new adventure. The main range of the Rockies, the Continental Divide, is a climatic barrier. The crossing of it brings one into a new world: the forest becomes denser and more moss-grown; sound, dry wood is harder to find; the wind has dropped, so that an unearthly silence pervades the meadows and the horses start to every sudden sound. Strange flowers make their bow, new trees are seen: the mountain ash, the western larch, the cedar. And, seen from the deeply incised valleys of the western slope, the mountains seem to tower to greater heights.

The rarest of all creatures to be met with on those western forays was man. But other British Columbians were there to

greet us on the borderline: at one crossing of the Divide we rode head on into a grizzly—and once, clambering up out of Alberta on a blazing summer afternoon, I stuck my head over the summit ridge of the Three Isle Lake mountains to find myself staring, at a few yards range, into the astonished countenance of a British Columbian goat. He was red with sandstone dust and he was hot and weary from climbing, and 5,000 feet below him I could see the shingle bars of the Palliser River. We gazed at one another for a moment in mute surprise; then the goat turned and loped away down the rocky slope, to vanish over some impossible precipice, leaving me perched on the backbone of the continent, alone with the silence and the sun.

Facing page: A scow on the Peace River.

That is the British Columbia of the high Rockies—but in the southern half of the province the Rockies are shared with Alberta. North of the Smoky River the Rockies belong entirely to BC, together with every living thing in their lonely meadows, east and west. There you will find the magnificent Stone sheep, merging slowly into Fannin's sheep and then the Dall. What other province, territory or state can show such wide variations in that most spectacular of beasts, the mountain sheep?

Go farther north and east. Cross the border into British Columbia by canoe as did the first white man, coming by way of the Peace River from the east, or by the Liard River from the Northwest Territories. There you will find a land of prairie, small forest and muskeg—a country cut by fast-running rivers, the old highways of the fur-traders.

What has this far northeastern plateau in common with the

gardens of Victoria, with Vancouver's lawns and flowering trees, with the silent inlets of the coast, the giant cedar and Douglas fir of Vancouver Island and the slow-crawling glaciers of the Coast Range? Nothing. The hard-riding stockman of the Chilcotin cattle ranges, the lumberjack and the fisherman of the coast, the fruit grower of the Okanagan—what do they know or care about this land beyond the Rockies? Nothing—and indeed less than nothing, for to most of them it is Ultima Thule, Siberia, the Land-that-God-Forgot: a wild man's country where only a wild man would care to live. Yet it is from that northeastern corner, till so recently the stepchild of official Victoria, that will flow the "black gold" and the natural gas that are today the stepping stones to fortune.

In that far country that drains to the Mackenzie you will find big grain fields, foothill cattle ranches, long traplines and lonely lakes where the migrating wild fowl pattern the autumn skies in ordered, wavering skeins. A prairie land—and in it you meet a certain type of man: a man created by the country in which he lives, by its wide horizons and its extremes of

Facing page: A "hard-riding stockman."

heat and cold, and by the fact that, almost alone of British Columbians, his vision is not limited by towering mountain ranges.

And then go elsewhere in the province—in fact, go anywhere you please between the Queen Charlottes and the Rockies or from Atlin Town to Trail—and, no matter in what valley or on what high plateau fate lands you, you will be certain to meet with some new, strange and interesting type of man. He will be sure to tell you—in his cabin, over his campfire, in his office—

about something that you have never heard of, never dreamed of before. He will tell it vividly, with a wealth of imagery and often with expressions that are far from parliamentary. Be wise and listen to him, for it is in sharing, perhaps for one night only, in this man's past that you will capture something of the endless variety of British Columbia.

A cougar hunter of Vancouver Island will tell you tales of terrorized west coast settlements and of children afraid to venture over the jungle paths that are cut through the dense tangles of salal. A fruit grower of the southern Okanagan will explain to you with lavish detail the economic value of the rattlesnake, the destroyer, he avers, of the mice who would otherwise strip the bark and kill his trees. The enthusiast who slaughters too many of these valuable reptiles is, you are made to realize, not a benefactor but a menace. A sheep herder of the Adams Plateau has wild tales to tell of the nightly visitations

of the grizzlies; a white-mustached old-timer, once a lineman on the old Yukon Telegraph Trail north of Hazelton, will tell strange stories of warped and bitter feuds over absurd trifles in the snowy silence of the northern bush. If you happen to sit next to a trained nurse on the northbound plane, and if she tells you that she is a full-blooded Haida from the Queen Charlottes, listen to her carefully for it is of the Viking past of her own people and of their raids and their red slaughters that she is talking. Listen (but not without discrimination) to a dude-wrangler of the northern plateau telling how the timber wolves and the grizzlies hang around his camps, waiting to snap up the cook of the outfit or some heedless, unarmed dude: it is always entertaining to hear a genuine artist laying it on with a shovel—especially when he thinks you are believing him.

Facing page: A pier at Tofino, on the west coast of Vancouver Island.

Go to some quiet country house on Vancouver Island if you want to get a connoisseur's verdict on an old Bukhara rug. And then go north to the great Stikine River. Go upstream to Telegraph Creek on one of the last of the BC riverboats and, as you go, listen to the talk of the rivermen and see for yourself, east of the Coast Range and far from salt water, a seal drive a mighty salmon out of the river and chase it across a dry shingle bar, each creature silhouetted and sparkling against the low morning sun.

Hear the old-timers while you may for they are departing, and the old life with them: no more will that well-remembered voice be heard, on the cool veranda of the most northerly ranch in BC, with the chuckle and rustle of Fizz Creek down below,

telling of the long haul of the winter mail by dog-team from Atlin to Telegraph Creek, of placer mining on the Dease, of digging for mastodon ivory.

See and hear all these things and many more besides. See the incredible hordes of a great salmon run jostling their way up the crowded Bulkley River; see the wild fowl flighting down the Rocky Mountain Trench. Turn, one by one, all the pages of the changeful book of the wilderness and know from it that man, inspired by nature's prodigality of invention, will build in British Columbia, in the fullness of time, cities and a people rich in their infinite variety. ▧

Facing page: Northern riverboats.

Liard River Voyage

The Beaver, Spring 1955

As our plane approached Fort Nelson, rents in the storm clouds gave us a sight of the country below and of the winding knot of rivers that come together there. Things didn't look so very good. The August rains of 1954 had done a thorough job: every hollow was a pool and every trail a morass while, of the rivers, the Sikanni Chief and the Prophet were running yellow with mud; the Muskwa alone seemed to be more or less clear.

At the airport the runways were still wet from the last downpour, and we—my cousin Christopher and myself—landed in a brief spell of watery sunshine, wondering why, in this so-called summer, we had been foolish enough to leave our homes.

The usual delays then fell to our lot, caused mainly by the impossible layout of the place. Alaska Highway Fort Nelson is ten miles southwest of the airport and the boat landing is nearly two miles in the opposite direction. Between the landing and Old Fort Nelson flows the Fort Nelson River, so the place is strung out over some 13 miles, with the river obstacle thrown in for good measure, and with a full-fledged Hudson's Bay Company store operating at the highway end of the line and an old-time Hudson's Bay Company post at the other end, beyond the river. The various facilities are scattered all over the map and, one way and another, anything more inconvenient it would be

Facing page: Jack Starke.

hard to find. However, eventually we got going and slipped away down the river in a sudden blaze of evening sunshine—sunshine that flattered only to deceive for, by midnight, it was once more raining.

The Fort Nelson River was misbehaving itself in a most unusual manner—it was in flood and still rising, in August of all seasons. Great uprooted trees and drift of all kinds went sailing by. Clots of yellow froth covered the stream and in the eddies the mud seemed to boil as if in a cauldron. It was best not to wash, or at least to wash only very prudently, since washing in this stuff merely made one dirtier, while drinkable tea could only be made by taking water from some clear side-stream. The wind swung into the northeast and the rain drove down out of the low, racing clouds. Photography became a waste of time and film and, after two days of this sort of thing, we camped in thick spruce opposite that old landmark of the voyageurs, Roche qui Trempe a l'Eau, and waited for the weather to clear. And one more day of rain went by.

With the slow unveiling of the sun, colour flooded back into a rain-washed world and, with it, hope. At midday we loaded up and that afternoon, shortly after passing the abandoned post of Nelson Forks, we came to the Liard and turned upstream. The canoe we were using was a 20-foot, Chestnut "Ogilvy Special," 36- by 13-inch square-ended, and to drive it we had a 5 ½-h.p. Johnson "Seahorse" 1954. We had left Fort Nelson with two 10-gallon drums of gas and that, with the Johnson's tank, gave us a maximum of 23.3 gallons, by now somewhat reduced. We intended to make it upstream some 70 miles to Hell Gate on the Liard, in the foothills of the Rockies. With us we had

R.G. McConnell's report on his descent of the Liard from the Lower Post in 1887 and the map he made on that trip, which, with its detailed information, is still, today, the best map of the Liard. What kind of water we should meet, however, we had little idea (it proved to be faster than we had expected), so, to conserve gas, we had come down most of the hundred miles of the Nelson with the paddle, and now we planned to track up the faster stretches wherever a good beach was available and to help the kicker along with paddle or pole if necessary. This system worked well and, since one's feet are usually wet when pushing a canoe upstream, it had the added advantage of keeping us limbered up and warm.

Somewhere in the far north and west, beyond the Rockies, the summer must have been a good one, for the Liard was running a faint silty green and a pail of its water was clear. Not only that, but the weather was perfect and it rained no more for nearly a month. Our troubles were over, all except one— we were overloaded, and when the kicker was running all out against fast water we had less than an inch of freeboard. So we cached some heavy stuff on an island and re-shuffled the load, and from then on all was well.

We worked our way up around the great bends where the Liard, crooked as a snake, races down through a maze of gravelly, wooded islands and sandbars, and one wonders which way to turn for the best. Low plateaus stood back from the river, and there was one view to the northwest, of the stony summits of the Mackenzie Mountains. Then those vanished behind nearer hills and we came to the Beaver River and turned up it for a couple of days, for the pleasure of travelling on a smaller stream. Its water was utterly clear and one longed for time to follow it for, far upstream and over several portages, there is a pass over the mountains that leads to the Meilleur River and to Deadmen's Valley on the Nahanni. An Indian's cabin and a well-built cache stood empty near the mouth of the Beaver: just above these and in a deep, quiet pool, we came on a black bear and two cubs swimming.

We went up the Liard, coping as best we might with the morning mists that are a feature of this river: they seem to come down about 5:00 or 6:00 A.M. on most days and can be so thick as to delay the start until 10:00 or even 11:00, so we travelled far into the evenings.

Extremely fast water soon gave place to a slacker current, and picturesque bluffs of sandstone and conglomerate rose sheer out of deep water on the southern shore. We came to a place where, for the first time, the mighty Liard is crowded together into one narrow stream between high cliffs; then we turned south into a long stretch of shale cutbacks and islands with swifter water than ever before and the two of us marched up the beaches, hauling on the trackline as the voyageurs of the Hudson's Bay Company used to do when the Liard was the only known route to the Cassiar country and the Yukon. That evening we camped in warm, dry spruce above a boulder beach and, under those trees, I was amazed to find one single, lonely plant of devil's club, that curse of the Selkirks and the Coast Range. I believe this is the first occasion on which it has been reported east of the Rockies.

Next day, toward midday, we hauled the canoe up a very strong riffle, which, we learned later, was Starke's Riffle, named after my old Klondiker friend of Nahanni days, Jack Starke. At the head of the riffle the Scatter River came in and in the bush below its lowest mouth, we saw a neatly painted sign—"No Admittance"—so, we landed. It was an abandoned prospecting camp of a season or two ago: the site was well cleared and a table for about eight and a cookstove still stood forlornly under the trees. A well-beaten trail ran to another site a little way off and there, nailed to a tree was a second painted board—"Office. 56 Church St." it said. So *that* was it—and a sudden vision came to us of bustling, hurrying men from a certain righteous eastern city, clad in gnome-like suits of sober hue and wearing on their heads those bowler hats that invariably provoke the West to mirth. Rackham, perhaps, could have caught this vision and set it on his canvas, with the amazed trees looking down. We elaborated on this theme and then, reduced to laughter, we withdrew from the sacred grove and boiled our profane tea-pail on the far side of the Scatter River.

That night we camped opposite Lepine Creek, named for W. Lepine whom McConnell met in 1887 making his way up the Liard with a crew of Company voyageurs toward the Dease River. "Lepine," writes McConnell, "had been employed on the river as a guide, in the old days when goods were taken by this route to the Yukon . . . [he] had become disheartened by the continued high water and the difficulties of up-stream navigation, and when we met him talked of returning, but we induced him to persevere."

From that camp it was only a short distance to the site of old Toad River Post, a couple of miles below the mouth of the Toad River. The site is on the north shore in the lee of a great cape of sandstone and shale. The buildings were still standing when McConnell passed by, though they had already been abandoned by the Company some time previously. Shoving through the jungle-like growth on the site I could find no trace of them— only, here and there in the ground, faint signs of excavations.

Five miles upstream we made camp where the clear, blue water of the Grayling falls into the Liard's green, and from our landing place we had the first close view of the northern Rockies—bare, brown summits against the cloudless evening sky. Late on the following day, with several small canyons behind us, we came to the foot of a strong riffle where the Liard swept at speed round a big island. Up it we went, the kicker running all out, climbing slowly the hill of racing water. At the head of the riffle, with tall cliffs on the right and a gravel beach with cliffs beyond it on the left, the current slackened; I cut the engine to a gentle hum and the canoe crept forward into a rock-walled mountain lake. I stared at my cousin and he stared at me. "My god," he said, "where's the Liard gone?"

I cut the engine out and in dead silence we drifted toward the right-hand shore. There was no sound of water ahead—all we could hear was the fading roar of the riffle we had left behind.

Ahead of us was an obvious camping place and we paddled toward it and threw the stuff out onto the beach; then we stood by the water's edge and looked and listened, but no sound came from this lake of, perhaps, 80 acres. It was evening now and the sun was shut off from this basin by the wooded hills and there were no shadows thrown; there was nothing to be seen

Facing page: A 30-foot boat driving upstream on the Liard River.

that might indicate current except the faintest of lines down the centre of the water. Quietly we got into the canoe and paddled away along the rocky shore. Supper could wait till we had found which way the river went . . .

Hell Gate is a narrow channel, with sheer walls, cut through an anticlinal ridge of limestone that crosses the river's path. On the left shore an older channel, also vertical-sided, is now abandoned except at high water, the two canyons thus making an island between them of water-worn rock, crowned with trees. The main channel of the Gate must be enormously deep: a strong riffle at its head caused the whole length of the Gate to be agitated by strong eddies and boils that, as we drifted past in the canoe, could be seen to rise and burst on the surface with considerable force, driving the water against the canyon walls. With care the Gate was passable for a canoe, but this was the end of the trail for us—we had an appointment with Nahanni Butte, some 240 miles downriver. And there was Albert Faille to find, and the Lower Rapids, close to Fort Simpson, to be photographed—there was no time to travel on by canoe into the canyon country. Instead, we would see all we could on foot.

We camped there, by the lagoon, for two days and three nights. The late afternoon of the second day found us some four miles up the Liard, at the foot of the next canyon. Rarely have I seen so beautiful a sight as this was at that hour. We lay among the dwarf spruce on a sun-warmed ledge high above the river, peering down into the canyon. Right out of the sun the Liard came. At the head of the gorge the tossing waves of a riffle flashed in the sunlight—

Facing page: Hell Gate on the Liard River, looking downstream.

they seemed to surge across the river and vanish into some rocky basin that we could not see. In the canyon itself, between its plunging walls, the boils and eddies writhed and twisted like silver snakes on the surface of the green water. Far ahead, the profile of a peaked and broad-shouldered mountain heaved up, outlined in the golden haze. It was a river idealized—a calendar picture of some artist's dream, but, this time, it was a dream come true.

With the warm smell of spruce and fir there came to us, now and then, the gentle splash of an eddy as it filled and spilled over, or the bubbling rush of some boil breaking on the surface. But that was all—no breeze was stirring on this hot September afternoon.

Through this canyon that lay below us there had passed many an expedition of the 1830s and 40s, sent out by the Company from Fort Simpson to explore the lands "beyond the Mountain." John McLeod had come this way, headed for Dease Lake and Terror Bridge on the Tooya River, and Robert Campbell, bound for Campbell's Portage and the Pelly. They passed not only once but many times, and at all seasons, and Dr. G.M. Dawson writes of them: "Less resolute men would scarcely have entertained the idea of utilizing, as an avenue of trade, a river so perilous of navigation as the Liard had proved to be when explored. So long, however, as this appeared to be the most practicable route to the country beyond the mountains its abandonment was not even contemplated. Neither distance nor danger appear to have been taken into account."

A minor tragedy marred our departure from Hell Gate. The Hudson's Bay store at Fort Nelson had not been too certain of the eggs that they had sold to us so, warning us of this, they had supplied an extra dozen free of charge. My cousin, egg expert to the expedition, had therefore broken each one separately into a cup but, so far, only one had been bad.

That made an odd number, and now there was only one egg left for breakfast: we eyed it hungrily and then tossed for it, and I won. Christopher broke the egg into a mug, recoiling slightly as he did so. Then he handed the mug to me with a grin spreading over his face—and I think that egg was more rotten, almost, than any egg has ever been. There is no moral that I can see to this story—it merely points out the infallibility of the Great Company. If they tell you there are rotten eggs about, then rotten eggs there will be and, as Long John Silver said, "you may lay to that."

On the way down we picked up our cached stuff at the island and dumped it again at the mouth of the Fort Nelson. There we had the good fortune to fall in with Dick Turner of the Netla River on his way down from Fort Nelson. "Throw your canoe onto my boat," he said, "and travel with me. You'll make better time." So we did that—and we tied up when darkness fell, at Francois' place. We sat late in the little cabin that night, listening to the gossip of the river from the Mackenzie to the Sikanni Chief, and the talk soon turned on Faille.

This time there was no hope, Turner said. It was over two years now since he had disappeared into his old hunting grounds in the Nahanni country, and no man, white or Indian, had set eyes on him since then. Even though he had done that sort of thing before—which he often had—that didn't mean he could go on doing it forever. No—a man gets old and then he makes a mistake, or the luck runs out . . . and we sat around the cabin table for a while in silence, thinking of the man who, in all likelihood, had been.

We came next evening to Dick Turner's trading post at the Netla River, 15 miles above the mouth of the South Nahanni and the first piece of news there, after the greetings were over, was that Albert Faille had been seen, alive and cheerful as ever, paddling down the Liard toward Fort Simpson. He was evidently out of gas and when hailed across the water and asked what had fetched him down from his mountains, he had shouted back, "Out of matches!"—as well he might be after 26 months—but, even so, that light-hearted reply was thought to conceal some deeper purpose.

Dick Turner had to make a flying trip to Fort Simpson and, knowing that I wanted to see Faille, he very kindly asked us to go with him—we could leave the canoe and outfit, he said, at the new post he was building at South Nahanni, close under the Butte. We could make the 110 miles in one day and get back in something under two, and that was a lot better than we could do with a canoe and outboard.

This was a godsend, and it is to this that we owe our pictures of the Lower Rapids of the Liard, taken from the middle of the river where we could never have ventured with a canoe. I had passed up and down these rapids in May and in July when they are buried deep by high water and nothing shows but a series of powerful swells, and I had tramped over them on snowshoes in February when nothing shows at all. But this was September, when the bones of rivers show: now we would see what all the fuss was about. R.G. McConnell, incidentally, refers to the Lower Rapids as merely "a series of strong riffles near the mouth of the Liard"—much to the indignation of the rivermen of today who cannot pass to and fro with their boats, through Shallow Bay and Driftwood Bay and over the reefs, as easily as the canoemen of 70 years ago could slip through the canoe channel along the right shore—portaging their outfits if the need arose, and lining down the empty canoes, which would ride high and light like autumn leaves on the surface of the water. McConnell, however, had just come down through the canyons of the Upper Liard and that, no doubt, tended to dwarf the Lower Rapids in his eyes.

Cape Island, between the Birch and Poplar rivers and over halfway to Simpson from South Nahanni, is the landmark for trouble, with a little fast water there; the rapids proper begin some seven miles lower down, with the mountains of the Nahanni Range fading from view for the last time at Poplar River. Turner piloted his boat, the *Come Later*, with skill and the knowledge born of experience, through the eight to ten miles of white and broken water, swinging from side to centre and back again, following the deepest channel.

The most spectacular chute is that of the Beaver Dam—a creaming line of white stretched across the Liard, which is here some three quarters of a mile wide. The boat channel in the Beaver Dam reef is about a quarter of the way out from the left shore. The river is continually changing here, and not for the better. The present passage through the reef opened about 1942 and, shortly afterwards, the canoe channel on the right bank became more difficult. We slipped easily down through the foaming water only to turn and head upstream again in mid-river till the bow of the boat was almost touching the reef: here, in 1951, two men out of three in a canoe were drowned trying to run straight up and over the Beaver Dam. We got our pictures, and then we dropped back and swung in to the eastern shore where we tied up, walking back upstream to the rapid. The sun blazed down out of a cloudless sky and the rocks were warm to the touch. Blue and white—the sliding rush of unbroken, falling water and the boiling cauldron at the foot of the slide—the Beaver Dam sprang out across the river, to be lost from view as it neared the farther shore. One could see low cliffs over there and, above them, groups of poplars that were already turning to their autumn gold . . .

Faille was at Fort Simpson and I found him there, early the next morning, sitting in his boat by the Mackenzie shore, tinkering with his outboard. A cold wind was blowing straight out of the rising sun, ruffling the surface of the mile-wide river. We talked over plans for the coming year and he told me where he would winter—he would be alone, he said, at the cabin that I knew, away back in the mountains of the Yukon Divide.

"Take care of yourself," I said. "Remember, we're not so young as we were when we first hit the Nahanni."

"No," he replied. "But you look pretty lively still and, Patterson, I don't aim to cash in yet. The main trouble is, we're not so quick as we were then—and that's what counts on a river."

A few days later I sat on the grass and the dead herbage of the summer's flowers, high up on Nahanni Butte. Here and there in the warm autumn sunshine the crocuses were blooming again, thinking it was spring; thunderstorms were creeping out of the mountains to the westward—they were still far distant and the sunlight poured down between them, stalking over the enormous country in shafts and pillars of gold. At the foot of the Butte, the Liard and the South Nahanni wound and twisted in great loops and oxbows: then they met and flowed away together into the flatlands toward the Mackenzie. To the southeast there was nothing, only the forested plain, but to the northwest could be seen the Twisted Mountain—one could almost lean forward and touch its russet slopes—and then the shining channels of the Nahanni until they vanished behind the Outpost Hills. Away beyond those hills I could see, bronze-coloured and glowing in the autumn sunlight, the sheep plateaus that rise above the Lower Canyon and, still farther, the mountain masses of the Tlogo-Tsho, shadowy and indistinct in the thickening haze—ghosts of mountains peopled with old and almost-forgotten ghosts.

Many a winter has come and gone since a McLeod set out from Fort Simpson with his men to go to the "Nahany lands." He made two trips and on one of those, according to the Hudson's Bay Company records, he and his party went only a short distance up the South Nahanni by canoe. Then they cached their canoes—it was flood time, so one can well understand why they did that—and went on, on foot. They "passed over nine ranges of mountains to a land in which there were no ranges, just detached mountains . . ." This can only have been the big, level alpine plateaus between the heads of the Ross and Gravel rivers—the country over which the Canol pipeline was laid during the last war. They had followed the Nahanni to its head and then gone on beyond—and still they had met with no Indians. However, they made contact with the Nahanis on their way back, "between the second and third ranges, counting from Fort Simpson," so this long and arduous journey was justified. Those trips were made by John M. McLeod in 1823 and in 1824.

All this happened so long ago that even the memory of those journeys faded, and in Ottawa—when Ottawa came to be—they knew them not, despite the fact that they are recorded in a published book of Canadian history. "Untravelled country" they called the South Nahanni, back east there in the holy of holies, and they retailed, to those seeking information, hair-raising rumours of the perils of that river—with the result that more than one would-be explorer deluded himself into the belief that he was "the first white man." But George Simpson's men had been ahead of these late-comers by over a hundred years, travelling in the interest of the Company. It would be an act of grace to place John McLeod's name, even so late in the day, in a commanding position on the map of the Nahanni country . . .

That evening the thunderstorms broke, and in the morning when we turned the canoe's nose up the Liard, the wind was in the north with a cold rain falling and big waves rolling up the river. On and off it rained for two days of varied travel and delay and then, on the third day, the sun blazed forth once more out of a tranquil sky. From our noonday fire I looked back down a long, blue reach of the Liard; in the far distance and cut off from all the nearer mountains there was something that caught the eye: it was low down on the horizon and it might almost have been a cloud—only there were no clouds on that splendid day.

It was Nahanni Butte—and it was faint and indefinite of outline because, on its upper slopes where we had climbed, there now lay a covering of freshly fallen snow. Round the next bend I looked back once more, but that had been the last of it—the trees were in the way now and the Butte was no longer to be seen. ▨

(Editor's note: Albert Faille lived on in the Nahanni country, trapping and prospecting, until he died at his cabin, in 1973.)

Peace River Passage

The Beaver, Winter 1956

In the whole stretch of the Rockies there is only one water passage through the heart of the range—that of the Peace River. Its two main heads are the Finlay and the Parsnip rivers. They, flowing in the Rocky Mountain Trench from the northwest and southeast respectively, meet in head-on collision at Finlay Forks—and in that moment the Peace is born. The Peace immediately turns away from the wide valley of the Trench that bounds the mountains on the west, and flows straight at the Rockies. It dives into the mountains and cuts its way through to the eastern plains; it followed that course ages before the Rockies rose across its path, and as they rose it cut them down, refusing to turn aside for them. One would expect the whole passage through the mountains to be barred with transverse reefs and cascades, but the river is amazingly tranquil. Two sets of strong rapids and numerous riffles have to be dealt with but that is all. The main barrier comes, not in the mountains, but almost 40 miles to the eastward, in the last ridge of the foothills—the Butler Ridge.

Facing page: The Peace River.

There, beneath that last spur of the ridge which in 1875 A.R.C. Selwyn, then Director of the Geological Survey, named Portage Mountain, the Peace passes through a "gate" in the rocks so narrow that one can fling a stone across it. That gate marks the plunge into the Rocky Mountain Canyon through which the

135

river becomes impassable, falling 225 feet in little over 20 miles. The portage trail follows what may have been a pre-glacial course of the Peace between Portage Mountain and Bullhead Mountain, rising high above the river. Mackenzie calls it the Portage de la Montagne des Roches. Selwyn explains carefully and somewhat pedantically in his report for 1875–76 that this name should be rendered Portage of the Mountain of Rocks and that it has nothing to do with the Rockies. But the misnomer was too old for him and Rocky Mountain Portage it has remained.

Such is the lay of the land and such the main obstacles on a river trip that must be unique in Canada. It must be a rare thing anywhere to be able to put one's canoe in the water beside a main highway, disappear into the wilderness and pass through a mountain barrier, and then, after 250 miles of downstream travel, return to a main road once more.

On September 10th, 1955, my wife and I loaded our canoe at Melville's on Trout Lake where the Hart Highway swings away toward Pine Pass and the Peace River country, leaving the rivers of the Rocky Mountain Trench. We ran across the four miles of lake under power, having brought with us a 3-h.p. Johnson for the few bits of upstream travel we might wish to make. People were rude to this small machine in that land of big

This page: Marigold Patterson at the head of the Peace River.
Facing page: The Parsnip River.

riverboats and 20- and 25-h.p. kickers—they called it an egg-beater and burst into laughter at the sight of it. Nevertheless it did all we asked of it, which was not much, as we had only burdened ourselves with five gallons of gas. Arrived in the lagoon at the outlet of Trout Lake, we shut off the outboard and shipped it so as to be able to enjoy the peace of this perfect autumn afternoon.

The eight miles or so of the Pack River between Trout Lake and the Parsnip ranked high in a trip that was full of beauty. No mountains were in sight, but this small, brown and very clear river, winding over gravelly shallows and tumbling down small boulder riffles, was a lovely thing to see. We took it lazily, delighted with the fall colours of poplar and cottonwood and the scarlet of the small brush along the banks. Ahead of us, down quiet reaches under the dark spruce, flew a family of

brown-headed ducks: we never quite caught up with them and we must have chased them for miles. Toward evening we slipped out into a Parsnip River that was low and shrunken and racing between wide shingle bars—a very different affair from the rolling flood that I had last seen in July, six years before. On our right the foothills and the mountains began to appear.

Life on the Parsnip seemed to be confined to prospecting parties coming out after the season's work. Two men passed by, heading upstream. The following day a gay-shirted party from the Ingenika appeared, lining up a riffle where the passage was so narrow that, if we had not pulled in to the bank and waited, a disastrous head-on collision would have ensued. The trackline, we noticed, was attached to the nose of the riverboat, from which we concluded that this was no expert crew.

Then came a day when camp was so pleasant that we stayed in it—and that was a piece of luck, for up the river came an old friend with the independent trader from Fort Grahame and an Indian. The frost was still white on the bars and there was a powdering of new snow on the Rockies that made it doubly pleasant to be able to serve out hot tea in a stove-warmed tent. We made no effort to hurry over that first hundred miles. Nevertheless we came, in the end, to the last reach of the Parsnip River on an evening of flaming sunset with crimson feathers of cloud floating high above the mountains of the Peace River Gap, and a riot of golden birches reflected in the quiet water.

In the morning we turned the egg-beater loose to see what it could do against the current of the Finlay. It did well: against some strong water it drove the 20-foot canoe up the four to five miles of river that lie between the actual forks and Pete Toy's

Bar where the McDougalls' post is situated. After tying up in the snye there, alongside the Forestry boat, I unshipped the kicker and shook it. Not a sound came; it had used exactly one tankful and had arrived on the smell.

The Finlay Rapids on the Peace River occur one mile downstream from the junction of the rivers, but the roar of them can be plainly heard from the McDougalls' post. We ran down to the head of the rapids on an afternoon of fantastic clouds that swirled around Mount Selwyn and boiled up in the Gap. We planned to run the rapids close in to the rocky south shore as we had run them in 1949, but snow squalls appeared in the Gap, trailing down from black storm clouds, and a cold northeast wind began to blow. We pulled in and made a well-sheltered camp where we could weather the storm, and from that camp we prospected the north shore in the morning.

P.L. Haworth and Joe Laurie went down that way in 1916 and this time we followed in their trail, slipping behind an island and then lining, wading and shoving the canoe down between rocks, through reefs and over falls. The last reef was impossible either to line around or run, but a magnificent sandy beach presented itself, over which we shoved the part-loaded canoe on rollers. This rapid is not difficult to run keeping close to the south shore, but on this occasion we had too much of a load and the wrong type of canoe.

We camped at the foot of the rapid in order to get some good pictures of Mount Selwyn, which was now partly snow-covered from the night's storm. This was the finest sight of the trip for me—the green and gold slopes of the mountain, leading up to the snow line and reflected in the river, and, to the westward,

the flashing water cascading over a half-mile of reefs, with the blue peaks of the far-off Wolverines as a background. Haworth found these rapids unimpressive. I cannot agree with him: the drive and uproar of the great river pouring across these barriers of schist was a memorable display of majesty and power.

The sun rose over the ridges of Mount Selwyn, shining through the hoar-frosted trees. The mountain towers 5.500 feet above the river. Selwyn himself made the first ascent on July 11th, 1875, with Professor Macoun, botanist to the Geological Survey expedition. They had been reading Sir William Butler's book and they had come half-expecting to find "the remarkable conical mountain, depicted in *The Wild North Land,* page 271." Reluctantly they concluded that the artist of that delightful book had drawn somewhat largely on his imagination, and they climbed the next best mountain they could find—the one that, from its position and shape, they thought Butler must have had in mind.

Facing page: Patterson at Finlay Rapids.

We loaded up and hit the river. The roar of the Finlay Rapids faded and we turned in to the mountains. We ran on, past Wicked River and past Bernard Creek to the Clearwater. In this short stretch of 30 miles we had passed through the main range of the Rockies.

A trail runs up the Clearwater; winding around enormous cottonwoods, avoiding small clumps of devil's club, that spiny curse of the western mountains, it comes in half a mile or so to the canyon, a famous fishing place. There were the fish—one could see them plainly down through the deep green water. And there they stayed—we had been told, six years ago (and had proved), that when the leaves begin to fall the fish of the Clearwater cease to take.

We ran on down to the Parle Pas Rapid, which marks the eastern edge of the mountains proper and the entrance into the foothill country. The full style and title is La Rapide qui ne Parle Pas, so named, says Warburton Pike, "from the absence of the roar of waters which usually gives ample warning of the proximity of a rapid." That may be so when the prevailing west wind is blowing; at other times the noise of the water can be plainly heard. The rapid consists of three reefs with actual falls on the south shore; the north side is a boulder chute with a very strong and very rough eddy at the foot. As before, we lined down the north shore—a proceeding that is apt to produce the sort of remarks that later on, sitting in amity by the campfire, both parties secretly regret. Little harm, however, has been done, since the noise of the water in the Parle Pas makes it quite impossible for the one on the line to hear the frantic directions and objurgations of the one on the pole—and vice versa.

A couple of miles below the rapid, the Ottertail River comes in from the north and, just above the junction and in the bank of the Peace, a dinosaur skeleton can be seen. We went on, through the Little Parle Pas, which is a series of powerful eddies, past lonely trapping cabins, past the Tepee Rocks, to Beatty's Landing close to Beatty's ranch. There we came upon that least likely of beings on this wild stretch of river—a man. He was leaning against a gate in the pouring rain, carrying a rifle, with a large dog at his heels. We pulled in and spoke with him, and arranged for Bob Beatty to be warned that two voyageurs begged

Facing page: Mount Selwyn.

to be freighted over the portage road in three days. And then we ran on down to Twelvemile Creek.

From this point it is 12 miles down to the head of the canyon. We ran down on a morning of deep blue sky and summer clouds; a powdering of snow lay on the Butler Ridge and the hills were lit with the flaring gold of the poplars. Portage Mountain loomed ahead, the landmark for the canyon, and the river increased its speed. We put ashore at Cust House, the old buildings of the Cust and Carey post where the old portage road comes down to the Peace. Below that the river has scooped out of the high cutbacks an amphitheatre that must be an eddying tumult of waters in flood time, though safe enough in the fall. We dropped down into it and came to the "gate" at the head of Rocky Mountain Canyon, to the place of the narrowing of the river and to the fantastic potholes in the rocks.

We lingered too long on the sun-warmed ledges of the canyon and evening caught us driving the canoe back toward Twelvemile Creek into the eye of a sunset that threw every swirl and eddy into full relief. The egg-beater could barely make it against that driving current; night was coming on and no camps offered. The sun set and the water took on the lemon colour of the sky, streaked with a swirling, shifting pattern of black. Facing page: "the remarkable conical mountain, depicted in *The Wild North Land.*" From low down on the water it seemed as if the river had gone futurist or else plain mad. Not until rocks and wave shadows had become as one did we make a desperate camp on an open bar, praying that it might not snow. Soon a fire blazed up on the stones and almost immediately a moose, disturbed in his beauty

sleep, began to grunt querulously from the farther shore. He was still querulous when he arrived in camp at 6:00 A.M. next morning. I set the porridge off the fire and slipped a cartridge into the Mannlicher, just in case—but the sound of the bolt seemed to turn him aside and he went on his way, slashing at the willows and grumbling to himself.

Bob Beatty turned up at Twelvemile Creek at the appointed time and in his capable hands we made a safe passage over a portage trail that had been freshly muddied by yet another rain. We decanted ourselves and the outfit on the beach below Hudson's Hope, slung the stuff into the canoe and paddled across the river to camp on the site of the old Rocky Mountain Portage establishment of the Hudson's Bay Company on the south shore. All that can be seen now are the faint excavations of old cellars, a few corner rocks and the half-buried mounds of chimney stones.

The forest, pioneered by young cottonwood saplings, is doing its best to take back its own. It is the beaver, appropriately enough, who is working overtime and preserving the site for the Company. We tripped over his cuttings as we made camp and several of him came to the edge of the firelight and banged loudly and resentfully on the darkly gleaming waters of the Peace.

Facing page: Marigold and Raymond Patterson, canoeing.

From that camp a long track of nearly two miles takes a canoe to the head of the strong riffle above "the Hope" and into the queer, narrow-based, rock islets that guard the lower end of the canyon. There we spent a day, returning to camp in the October dusk with the canoe leaping over the waves of the long riffle and the lights of Hudson's Hope already twinkling on the cliffs of the north shore. And in the greyness of the morning we departed from that place, bound for the Lower Gates of the Peace and the 50-mile run downstream to the Alaska Highway bridge. 🔲

With Butler on the Omineca

The Beaver, December 1952

▨ Out of doors the snow of a hard winter lay deep. Yet for the small boy who was sprawled in front of the library fire, all was warmth and comfort; the book that lay open, its pages held down by a billet of apple wood, was Sir William Butler's *The Wild North Land,* and the boy was far away by other snows, alone by his campfire on the banks of the mighty Peace River. "The fire lit up the pine stems," said Butler, "and the last glint of daylight gleamed in the western sky." So it did here, in the north of England—and through a belt of pines, too, appropriately enough, that lay beyond the tennis lawn. Arched over the sunset was the gleaming crescent of the Daylight Comet, for it was January in the year of the two comets, 1910: Halley's Comet also was due to pay Earth one of its infrequent visits.

The pages turned to another illustration. There they were again, Butler and his party, cutting up a moose on a shingle bar. It was spring now and the Peace was open, but snow still adhered (heaven and the artist alone knew how) to the almost-vertical slopes of a cone-shaped mountain—a mountain so extraordinary that no less a man than A.R.C. Selwyn himself, then Director of the Geological Survey, went to look for it and Facing page: The house in the north of England in which Patterson grew up. mentions it in his report for 1875–76: "At each turn of the river we expected that [it] would break upon our vision. In this, however, we were destined to be disappointed . . ."

Next picture? "Running stern foremost the Black Canyon."
What a place! Beneath those frowning crags the wild river seemed
to come alive and the canoe to move in the flickering light of
the fire. Decidedly a place for the boy to go and see, as soon
as he was big enough to handle a canoe. In the meantime, just
reading about it would have to do—and the "campfire" received a
vigorous bash from the poker that made it leap into flame . . .

Forty years went by and then, in September of 1949, I found
myself running a 16-foot canoe down the Finlay River from the
Fishing Lakes and Fort Ware. Now at last, for the Black Canyon!
And on September 3rd I ran the canoe into the mouth of the
Omineca and made camp. The morning of the 4th was perfect,
and I loaded up, flicked the canoe out into the current on the
end of the trackline and started to walk up the bars.

That resolute and indefatigable man, R.G. McConnell, had
made an exploration of the Omineca in 1893. For the first 35
miles, he says, until quiet water is reached 9 miles above Little
Canyon, the river drops 425 feet, with an average fall of 12 feet
to the mile. McConnell also comments on the huge driftpiles
of the Omineca. The Finlay, I thought, had gone the limit in
piling up these obstacles to navigation, but I soon found that
the Omineca, in proportion to its size, was far worse. For a
whole long day I poled, lined and "frogged"
the outfit up the river, shoving the canoe and
load over a huge cottonwood, around which
there was no poling bottom, portaging the
outfit up a sandbar in the middle of the stream at a point where
dangerous driftpiles lined both banks. Luckily it was warm, for

Facing page: The head of
the Black Canyon.

"frogging," in Finlay River parlance, means wading the canoe upstream, yourself sometimes waist deep in the fast water.

The Black Canyon is some eight or nine miles up from the mouth, and evening was coming on when I rounded a bend into a beautiful reach, free from driftpiles with a good tracking beach. There seemed to be cliffs in the distance, golden yellow cliffs; they came closer, and then the current slacked off and I took the paddle for the first time that day and nosed up into the canyon. I had been a longish time on the way—just on 40 years—but I still could not improve on my awed comment of 1910: "What a place!"

I dropped back to the mouth of the canyon and made camp in the dead silence of the quiet water, on the fine gravel of an old bed of the Omineca; it had changed its course a few years before in a tremendous flood, bursting through a wall of tall old spruce that may have seen Butler go by, and leaving high and dry its old channel. The weather was perfect so the lean-to was set dead facing the North Star, to provide shade for the grub and outfit at noonday.

Here, but on the opposite bank of the river, Butler camped on May 11th, 1873. The river then was high and swift with the spring run-off and things seemed decidedly tough. "We looked," he says, "a moment at the grim gate which we had to storm on the morrow, and then put in to the north shore, where under broad and lofty pines, we made our beds for the night"

Any forebodings that they may have had were more than justified. The weather in that May of 80 years ago was "hot and fine," and the heat was melting the mountain snows. The Omineca was rising fast—on the night of the 13th, for example, it rose two feet—and the difference, in a narrow gut like the Black Canyon, half a mile long and varying in width from 100 to 200 feet, between the calm tranquillity of September and the foaming torrent of May and June, can easily be seen. At the head of the canyon I found indications of a 30-foot rise from the September level.

Butler and his three co mpanions set forth into the Black Canyon on the morning of May 12th and crawled up in the eddies under the cliffs. "In the centre ran a rush of water that nothing could stem. Poling, paddling, clinging with hands and nails to the rock: often beaten back and always edging up again, we crept slowly along."

Facing page: Portaging the canoe.

They came, at the end of a morning's work, to the foot of a "wild cataract of foam," halfway through the canyon. Here there is a

very steep portage trail up a coulee in the canyon wall, rising over 160 feet, and up this trail in the sweltering heat they carried their camp and outfit to the head of the canyon, the canoe being too heavy to portage.

They came back for that, and from the foot of the portage trail for a little way upstream a certain amount of beach made tracking easier. But after dinner they wallowed forward, half in the river, half on the rocks of the shore, lining, pulling and shoving the canoe. The beach on the north shore then came to an end and they were faced with a desperate crossing—a straight shoot across a wild rush of water in the centre of the canyon to try and catch a small eddy on the south shore. If they missed that small eddy they would be swept backwards against the cliffs and into the worst rapid in the canyon; it was the old, old game of "catching the eddy" and, as usual, the longer they looked at it the less they liked it. So they tried it: they drove in their paddles, there was a bewildering whirl of water and "a wild yell of Indian war-whoop from Kalder," and in a couple of seconds they were safely across. On they went, lining from rock to rock, till they reached the foot of the last fall and the stiffest one: above this and on the far shore lay their camp and outfit.

Here disaster struck. Butler, with two men, floated a line back, round a massive promontory, to Kalder who was holding the canoe in the eddy. This line Kalder made fast to the nose of the canoe and a second line also, which he coiled loosely round his waist. Then he nosed the canoe out of the eddy into the current with a long pole. And then everything happened in a flash—the men up above hauled, the canoe sheered out into the flood, and the upper line broke. The full weight now came on Kalder who extricated himself from the coils by a miracle, grabbed his line and hung on. His line snapped and away went the canoe, taking with it their meat and tent. "We crouched together on the high rock, which commanded a long view down the Black Canyon, and gazed wistfully after our vanishing boat." Night was coming on, they had no axe, no grub and no canoe, and camp was on the wrong side of the Omineca.

They walked back to the lower end of the canyon and, while Butler and two men set to work to construct a raft out of the logs of an old cache, Jacques, the miner, who had no faith in the raft idea, went on downstream to look for the canoe. The party of three somehow managed to get across, the raft going to pieces on an island, and made their way back to camp, to a well-earned supper and to bed.

Early next morning, May 13th, they heard Jacques shouting from the far side. The canoe was on an island four miles below the canyon and not much the worse—a wonderful piece of luck.

more to the canyon mouth, determined "to seek through the Parsnip River an outlet to the South."

However, their luck had turned. Just below the canyon mouth and on the right bank they caught sight of gaudily coloured blankets, and landed hastily to find a pile of gear—traps, beaver, flour—and a pair of miner's boots, which Jacques, after careful examination, decided must belong to the Cornish miner, Pete Toy, who was evidently portaging his stuff down from the upper to the lower end of the canyon. Pete soon appeared carrying a huge load, and when greetings and news had been exchanged he set to and cooked the sodden voyageurs a right royal feed. All was soon arranged: Pete's canoe was above the canyon and theirs was below. "Happy coincidence! We would exchange crafts: Pete would load his goods in our boat, and we would once again carry our goods to the upper end of the canyon, and there, taking his canoe, pursue our western way." So they set out, late in the evening, "to stagger for the last time to the west end of the portage," and next morning they were on their way toward the gold-mining settlements of the upper Omineca. "Behind us lay the Black Canyon, conquered at last; and as its sullen roar died away in the distance . . . I drew a deep breath of satisfaction—the revulsion of long anxious hours."

In that way Captain W.F. Butler (as he then was) dealt with the Black Canyon—an incident in his long and adventurous journey from Fort Garry to Quesnel and Victoria in 1872–73, all so vividly described in *The Wild North Land.*

And now it was 1949; sunset was deepening into twilight, and supper was still to get. Butler and Pete Toy and all those heroes of an earlier day were memories now, and the story of

Down they went again to the canyon mouth where they built a big, strong raft, picked up Jacques, and so reached the canoe. By evening it was landed once more behind the rock from which they had made their famous crossing of the previous day. The sun blazed down, the cottonwood leaves were coming green and, that morning, they had seen the first hummingbird in camp. And the Omineca was rising fast.

On the 14th, after breakfast, they went back to the canoe, this time with a decided feeling of uneasiness. They shot out of the eddy to make the crossing, but now the increased weight of water was too much for them. "There was a moment's wild struggle, during which we worked with all the strength of despair. A second of suspense, and then we are borne backwards . . . until with a rush as of wings, and amid a roar of maddened water, we go downwards toward the canyon's wall."

As Butler says, they might as well have tried to stop an express train: they smashed into the cliff and split the canoe to the centre, but it still somehow held together. "And now, ere there was time for thought, we were rushing, stern foremost, to the edge of the great rapid." And this must have been the moment immortalized for posterity by the Victorian artist in his splendid conception of the Black Canyon.

But it was not the end. They went over the drop, the white water surged and hissed around them and the canyon walls whirled by—and in a few seconds they were safely down in the quiet eddies, soaked, half swamped and, for a while, bereft of speech. They held a council of war. To try the canyon a third time, they decided, would be a folly after this escape: wearily, they portaged their outfit back to the canoe and ran down once their deeds and their endeavours and their high courage was an old tale that would stir the blood and quicken the heart for generations to come. Soon the fire smoke was drifting out onto the quiet river (it must have been close to this very spot that Butler and his men enjoyed "the feast of Toy") and the scent of trout and bacon was rising from the pan. During supper a great round moon shouldered its way out of the Peace River Gap in the Rockies and climbed into the sky over Mount Selwyn, and when all was finished and put away, I walked down to the water's edge and looked up into the Black Canyon—a study in black and silver, broken only by the pale moonlit gold of the little birch trees on the ledges. There was no movement save, here and there, widening rings in the black water—no sound save the gentle lap and fill of some deep eddy . . .

R.G. McConnell, whose place is among the greatest of the explorer-surveyors, had a healthy respect for the Black Canyon, and writes of it in his report: "In low water the navigation of the Canyon is reported to be easy, but in seasons of flood the swollen stream is partly dammed back, and its effort to force a way through the narrow channel is attended with the production of such whirlpools and billows that its passage with large boats is exceedingly difficult and with small boats impossible." McConnell and his men portaged—not the short canoe portage that Butler had made, but the full-length portage, also on the north bank and next morning, after breakfast, I paddled across to find the portage trail.

Up a steep creek coulee it went, and a message cut on a tree showed that three men had dragged their boat over it in July of this same year, and a nice job that must have been, even with skids and rollers and block and tackle, for the trail rises some 160 feet before dropping again to river level in its half-mile of length. The descent to the river at the upper end is gradual, ending over sloping rock—and there, above any normal high water, a canoe was cached, set around with a stout little corral of logs to keep it safe from falling trees, or from a playful slap from some passing bear. A dwarf Michaelmas daisy made this head of the portage into the gayest of rock gardens; to the west the Wolverine Mountains showed fresh and clear-cut in the light of the rising sun, and on the portage trail every twig and every autumn leaf glittered under the heavy dew.

Across the river and a little way downstream was a deep bay between rocks, piled high with enormous banks of golden sand. There, next day, I found the ruins of a cache, sluice boxes and flume—and, upright, forlorn and immovable, a great slab of golden schist, the fireback of the fireplace of a vanished cabin, swept away, I was told later on, in the great high water of 1948; it had also, it seems, floated the canoe out of its log corral at the head of the portage and laid it high up in the bush.

I walked back to the canoe, paddled across to camp for fishing tackle and a tea-pail, and headed up into the Black Canyon. Time lost its meaning in that place of quiet waters. The sun rose and set, and one golden day followed another, and still the canoe lingered in that enchanted spot, passing from the eddy to the stream and back again, even as the trout and Arctic grayling did down in the clear depths, playing along the shadow line. Sometimes there would come, stealing down the canyon, the very faintest whisper of a breeze: warm, scented

Facing page: The Black Canyon at noon.

with autumn and the clean smell of pines. Down would flutter a red leaf from a choke cherry or a golden leaf from one of the little birch trees that glowed on the ledges like so many Chinese lanterns. The red and gold leaves would drift lazily on the green water, and the ripples, stirred by the breeze, would set their bars and patterns of light climbing the gleaming walls of mica schist in a maze of flashing colour. And then all would be still again except for the drip of water from the paddle or the drowsy chuckle of an eddy as it filled and overflowed.

And you can have the wild, magnificent canyons of the Nahanni, I thought, and you can keep the gay, sunlit reaches of the Dease, and the wide Stikine with its great, snow-capped mountains. Just give me the little Black Canyon of the Omineca and make it always autumn . . .

Then came an evening when faint mares' tails appeared in the northeastern sky. Dusk showed long black clouds racing along the Rockies, and in the night it poured. Breakfast was a wet, cold, smoky hell, and a freezing rain drove down straight out of the north—and what could a man do but curl up under the lean-to and mend his moccasins and read? But it eased up in the afternoon and the sun peered forth again, though a wild battle of inky clouds was still raging round Mount Selwyn.

I loaded up and ran for it down the racing Omineca. The wind was rising now and blowing sand off the bars, and twice a whirlwind caught me and spun the canoe end for end. And then the wind dropped and the clouds vanished, and I came again to the Finlay. I turned and looked back toward the Wolverines, utterly clear and sharp against a frosty sky. Somewhere in that direction lay the shadowy, gleaming paradise of the Black Canyon.

Well, it was gone now, vanished like a dream—like the fabled Garden that the Old Man of the Mountain made at Alamut. Now for something new—and I turned the canoe's nose downstream toward Finlay Forks and the Peace River Gap. ▨

THE R.M. PATTERSON COLLECTION

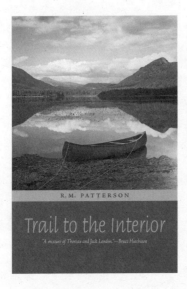

R.M. PATTERSON

Trail to the Interior

"A mixture of Thoreau and Jack London."—Bruce Hutchison

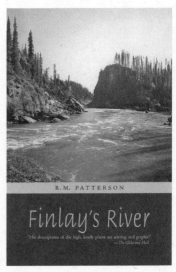

R.M. PATTERSON

Finlay's River

"His descriptions of the high, lonely places are stirring and graphic."
—The Globe and Mail

Few men have been as set on isolated adventures and as passionate about the wild landscape of Canada as R.M. Patterson. He spent over 30 years in exploration, from the northern rivers such as the Nahanni and the Liard, to his foothills ranch in the Rockies, and he recorded his discoveries entertainingly in words and photographs along the way. He travelled to the edges of settled Canada, armed with little more than a canoe, tarp and tea pail, and his words are imbued with the spirit of first sight. In many a clearing or teetering on a hilltop, Patterson committed his experiences to the page, capturing the purity of space, and shaping our collective imagination of the Canadian wilderness.

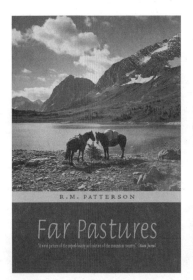
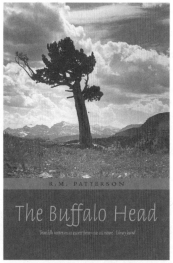

Born in 1898, R.M. Patterson spent most of his life pursuing adventure in the Canadian West. He is one of Canada's first and most beloved outdoor-adventure writers. Each of TouchWood's new editions of his classics features a foreword by Patterson's daughter, Janet Blanchet, providing an intimate, unique perspective on her father and his writings.

Trail to the Interior: 978-1-894898-50-8 / $19.95 pb
Finlay's River: 978-1-894898-38-6 / $19.95 pb
Far Pastures: 978-1-894898-15-7 / $19.95 pb
The Buffalo Head: 9778-1-894898-16-4 / $19.95 pb